Rising to Common Ground

Rising to Common Ground

Overcoming America's Color Lines

Ecumenical Edition

Danny Duncan Collum

Sowers Books
Louisville, Kentucky

Book design by Kirkby Gann Tittle
Cover design by P. Dean Pearson

First edition

Published by Sowers Books and Videos, a division of JustFaith, Inc.
Louisville, Kentucky

ISBN 978-0-9765203-3-7

PRINTED IN THE UNITED STATES OF AMERICA

06 07 08 09 10 11 12 13 14 15 — 10 9 8 7 6 5 4 3 2 1

Contents

Preface

Anyone who attempts a discussion of race in the United States today must begin with the definition of terms. In the last century, the American concept of "race" was mostly a matter of black and white. If your ancestors were from anywhere in Europe, you were "white." If you had any evident African ancestry, you were "black." There were Asian-Americans on the Pacific Coast and in big-city "Chinatowns," Mexican-Americans in the Southwest, scattered pockets of Native Americans around the country, and later Puerto Ricans in the urban Northeast. But those were local variations on the national theme. When you said "race," everyone knew that you were talking black and white.

Then, near the end of the twentieth century, America began to experience a great new wave of non-European immigration. Most of the immigrants were coming from Latin America, especially Mexico and Central America. Many were coming from Asia and the Middle East. As we will see in this book, earlier waves of European immigrants had been, upon arrival, encouraged to shed their national or ethnic identities and enter America's racial hierarchy. For those immigrants, to become American was to become "white." But few of our new immigrants pass the old skin tests for either "white" or "black."

More than one hundred years ago, the African-American sociologist, W.E.B. Du Bois, wrote that the question of the twentieth century would be the "question of the color line." And so it was. But at the start of the twenty-first century, America has a plurality of color lines.

Still, this book will talk about "race" in America first as a matter of black and white. I agree with Rev. Eugene Rivers that questions of "color" in America grow mainly from the root experience of African slavery, the struggle over slavery, and its aftermath (see *Sojourners,* March–April, 1998). That was the race issue that dominated the first two centuries of American politics. It hovered over the nation's founding, gave rise to the ideology of white supremacy, and led to our bloodiest war. This race issue has served to define the boundaries of our democracy. We have only begun to address it in the past fifty years, and then only in fits and starts. A four-hundred-year-old problem is not likely to be solved by fifty years of part-time effort. The first part of this book shows how the legacy of African enslavement lingers among us today.

This is, of course, not to suggest that Africans were the only "nonwhite" people subjected to racism from the earliest days of American history. Racist mythologies were certainly deployed to justify the dispossession and near-genocide of the country's indigenous people. Their suffering was at least as horrible as that of blacks under slavery, and so are its continuing effects. Hispanics began to be part of the U.S. in significant numbers in the 1840s, with the conquest of the northern Mexican territories that are now our Southwestern states. The Mexicans too were an occupied and often dispossessed nation, subject to widespread discrimination and systematic injustice.

But the experience of those groups to whom America came uninvited was different in one important way from the experience of enslaved Africans. The people of the indigenous nations and the conquered Mexicans retained a national identity that reached back before the U.S. They were subjected to discrimination and forced to learn and use English. The native peoples especially were victims of a cultural genocide, even after their numbers and territory were pitifully reduced. But even in the worst times, even the native people of America owned their own bodies, could name their ancestors, and had the freedom to form families of their choosing. Enslaved Africans lost all of that and then lived under those conditions, generation after generation, for two hundred years—from the 1600s to 1865—during the founding and formative years of our nation. There is no precedent or parallel for that experience. It affected everything about our country, and it still does.

Today "nonwhite" immigrants—Hispanic, Asian, and Middle Eastern—are more numerous than African-Americans. But these new arrivals are being incorporated into a highly racialized culture—organized along black-white lines—that has existed for almost four hundred years. Their presence will modify America's racial structure, but it will not suddenly eliminate that structure. Understanding the history and significance of African enslavement and oppression and the racial ideologies that grew up to justify it will continue to be essential for understanding America, at least through the rest of this century.

To further define our terms, the imagined audience for this book is American Christians, or even more specifically, white American Christians. Black Christians don't need me to tell them about race. Hispanic, Asian, and Middle Eastern Christians have their own story to tell, though they may benefit from this book's review of U.S. racial history and racial dynamics. However, Jesus said that the physician should go to the one who is sick. We white people are the often unwitting carriers of the white supremacist virus in America. We are the ones responsible for counteracting it and stopping its spread.

For some of us, our family histories in this country go back to the time of slavery. We may have had ancestors who opposed slavery or who owned slaves. Mostly likely our forebears were part of the silent majority that tolerated the existence of slavery and the regime of systematic segregation and disenfranchisement of blacks that continued into the late 1960s. Silence about these sins of racism, past or present, means complicity in them, just as surely as if we witnessed a murder and chose not to call the police.

On the other hand, many white Americans are descended from European immigrants who came to this country during the century between the Irish famine and World War II. Those immigrant ancestors played a small part, or none at all, in the struggles involving slavery. Most of them lived in parts of the country with small black populations. They often struggled to overcome nativist prejudices and assimilate into white America. That assimilation process provided them with little help in seeing the relationship of their story to America's racial structure.

As this book will show, those stories are connected. For nearly four hundred years, American struggles for justice for workers and low-income communities have been entwined with the struggle for racial unity and equality. When the races have been divided or turned against each other, working families of all ethnicities have suffered.

We come to this study as Christians. Our Christian faith provides us with the best prism for viewing the paradox of race in America today. It teaches us that all human lives are equally worthy and sacred. It teaches us that every race, culture, and nationality is included in God's work to redeem the Creation. It commands us to act for justice and to make the cause of oppressed people our own.

In this book, we will look at race from the angles of biblical theology, Christian tradition, history, economics, psychology, and culture. By the end, we will try to arrive at an approach to thinking, speaking, and acting about race that integrates those insights and suggests a way forward. It is my hope that this book will provide some aid to my fellow Christians in becoming part of the solution to America's racial injustice and division in the twenty-first century.

Finally, a personal note is unavoidable here: I am a white

Southerner and a Christian. In my native land, the Southern Baptist church in which I was raised provided the religious backbone for the system of segregation and the ideology of white supremacy. However, in my Mississippi hometown of Greenwood, the witness of a few brave ministers, priests, and white laypeople who joined the black community in marching for civil rights showed me another way to be Christian. I believe that American Christians can play a role in positive racial change, and I believe it for the same reason that Mark Twain believed in infant baptism: I have seen it done.

Chapter 1

Does Race Still Matter?

Whenever a discussion of racism arises—for instance around the continuing use of affirmative action—someone is sure to say that racial discrimination in America is a thing of the past. "We dealt with that forty years ago," goes the complaint. "So why does it keep coming up?"

It is an understandable perception. A lot has changed in America in the past forty years. In one amazing five-year period, from 1963 to 1968, the African-American civil rights movement achieved its national legislative goals. New laws banned racial discrimination in public facilities, employment, voting rights and housing. The Southern system of racial segregation, called "Jim Crow," was dismantled; and the large population of Southern blacks began to vote freely for the first time since the end of Reconstruction in 1877.

Most white Americans encounter blacks most often through television, and there, too, the picture has changed since the 1960s. African-Americans appear as reporters and anchors on the news, as central characters in entertainment programs, and as representative faces in advertisements. If you live in a predominantly white suburb (as most white people do) and have the outside world piped in through a fiber-optic cable, you could convince yourself that America is now one big happy rainbow family.

But the reality is that race still matters—a lot. America is a very different place for African-Americans than it is for whites. By every possible measure of health, income, and education, our country, on average, simply works better for white people.

Black and White Numbers

The difference between black and white in America can be tracked from the cradle to the grave. According to the U.S. Department of Health and Human Services, the black infant mortality rate is more than twice that for white infants. Meanwhile, the life expectancy of African-Americans lags far behind that of whites. A black man born in 1999 is expected to live to the age of 67.8, while a comparable white man will live to be 74.6. A black woman is expected to live to the age of 74.7, while her white counterpart can expect to reach 79.9 (Joint Center for Economic and Political Studies).

During their adult years, African-Americans are much more likely than whites to be poor or unemployed. As this is written, the unemployment rate for white men is about five percent. For black men it is 10 percent. For more than 20 years, black unemployment has ridden at a consistent five to six percent above the white rate. The poverty rate for white families is nine percent; for African-American families it is 23 percent. And the income gap persists even for families who do make it out of poverty. Median household income for blacks is consistently about 58 percent of the white median. Most recently the figure was $54,000 per year for white families, versus $33,000 for blacks (The Congressional Black Caucus Foundation).

Crime rates always go up with poverty and unemployment. It should be no surprise that the latest statistics from the U.S. Department of Justice show that 765 of every 100,000 black men are currently in prison, compared to 160 of every 100,000 white men. In fact, according to a study published by the American

Sociological Association, more young African-American men have served prison time than have enlisted in the military or earned a college degree. The researchers found that 20 percent of all black men born from 1965 through 1969 had served a prison sentence by the time they reached their early 30s. By comparison, less than 3 percent of white males from the same age group had done prison time.

Education is touted as the path to upward mobility in America. But the numbers indicate that the education system isn't working much better for African-Americans than is the economy. From the early elementary grades on up to graduate school admission, black students consistently score below comparable white students on the standardized tests that are used to measure academic achievement and potential. Overall, as reported by the PBS program *Frontline*, on standardized tests the average black student scores below 70 to 80 percent of the white students the same age. And the gap is not only seen in test scores. Seventy-four percent of all American teenagers graduate from high school on time. But only 56 percent of blacks do. Of the black males who manage to graduate from high school, only 53.4 percent finish college, compared to 64.5 percent of white males.

So, at the end of the education pipeline, it's no surprise to find that African-Americans are underrepresented in the highest-paying professions. For instance, blacks, who are 13 percent of the U.S. population, make up only 3.9 percent of all lawyers, according to the American Bar Association. The National Medical Association, an organization of African-American doctors, estimates that only 3 to 5 percent of U.S. doctors are black.

These numbers and dozens more like them point to something deep, powerful, and pervasive in American life that functions to the disadvantage of black people. It's something we can call *structural* or *systemic* racism, and it has easily survived the legal reforms and cultural changes of the past forty years. And the statistics of black poverty and marginalization are self-perpetuating. Many black children grow up in a world in which the people with wealth and high status simply don't look like them and in which the people who do look like them are poor or in prison. We shouldn't be surprised if they use this information to begin forming expectations about their own lives. At the same time, white children may observe the correlation between low status and dark skin in the world around them and, if no one offers another explanation, they may logically assume that there is simply something "wrong" with dark-skinned people.

The effects of these stereotypes in people's lives can be measured. Social psychologists at Stanford University studied the effect of racial attitudes and anxieties on students' standardized test scores. For instance, they had two groups of white students take a math test. One group was told that the test was simply a research tool. The other group was told that the test was one upon which Asian students excelled. The second group performed more poorly. When black students took the test, one group was again told that it was simply a research tool. The second group of black students was told that the test would measure their intellectual ability. Again, the second group had significantly lower scores. The researchers concluded that student performance was affected either by the internalization of stereotypes about black intellectual capacity, or by anxiety about confirming those stereotypes. They also found that the test score difference was greatest among high-achieving African-American students who might be expected to feel the most pressure to disprove stereotypes about their academic ability.

Racism: A Social Sin

These racial inequalities in American life have persisted through decades in which legal limits on African-American aspirations were removed. At the same time, cultural norms about race were changing, too. In recent decades, students of public opinion have found that the individual attitudes of white Americans have moved steadily away from overt racial bias and toward affirming the principles of racial equality.

However, legal reform has not been enough to establish justice for African-Americans. Changing the personal attitudes of white Americans has not done it either. That's because American structural racism is something that goes much deeper than either law or individual prejudice. For Christians, the structural racism of American society can be said to constitute a "social sin." Succinctly, social sin arises when people copy or cooperate with one another in allowing and promoting sin. This is often evident in what becomes socially acceptable or what is institutionalized in the social structure or laws. Thus slavery and child labor were social sins, even when they were legal and socially acceptable practices.

In the early twentieth century, Protestant theologians of the "social gospel" tradition, such as Walter Rauschenbusch, developed a doctrine of social sin that was rooted in the historic doctrine of original sin. Christians affirm that we all participate in the sin of Adam and Eve. Even if we do not sin by choice, the effects of original sin are transmitted to us in our divided and self-seeking human nature. Therefore, Rauschenbusch noted, all the social and economic institutions created by human beings are also distorted by sin and may become impersonal agents for the spread of sin.

In the 1960s, William Stringfellow, an activist attorney and Episcopal lay theologian, sharpened the analysis of social sin for many Christians by drawing on the language of "powers and principalities used by St. Paul (see especially Colossians 1:15–20). Bill Kellermann reports that in an address to a 1963 meeting of the Commission on Religion and Race, Stringfellow identified these powers and principalities as ". . . the great institutions and ideologies active in the world." Stringfellow maintained that:

Racism is not an evil in human hearts or minds; racism is a principality, a demonic power, a representative image, an embodiment of death, over which human beings have little or no control, but which works its awful influence in their lives. . . . It is the power with which Jesus Christ was confronted and which, at a great and sufficient cost, he overcame. In other words, the issue here is not equality among human beings, but unity among human beings. . . . The issue is the unity of all humanity wrought by God in the life and work of Christ.

For more than three hundred years the sin of racism was allowed to work its awful influence" in American society. It has now become exceptionally difficult to remove. Social sin, like any other sin, requires confession and repentance. Once we become aware of it, we are obligated as Christians to avoid participating in it as individuals—even by our silence. We are instead required to use any just means available to us to change the structures of sin and to bring our society into closer conformity to the norms of the Kingdom of God, in which, to paraphrase Galatians 3:28, there is neither black nor white.

The rest of this book will try to show how the social sin of racism functions in American society, the ways that we white Americans participate in it, and some ways we could begin to act constructively to make our society more just for everyone.

Chapter 2

What Is Racism?

We should be clear that when we talk about racism, we are not talking merely about ordinary stereotypes and prejudices. All over the world, throughout all of history, people have held uninformed negative opinions about their neighbors. The British and French, the Vietnamese and Chinese, the Colombians and Mexicans all do it. This human foible of stereotyping may sometimes be hurtful and may exacerbate real conflicts, but it usually doesn't serve to justify one group's total physical, psychological, economic, and cultural power over another. That is racism.

We can define *racism* as prejudice coupled with power for the purpose of domination. For example, the European anti-Semitism of past centuries fit this description. The stronger group (Christians) used their anti-Jewish prejudices to justify the oppression and segregation of Jews, to inspire violent attacks on their communities, and to drive Jews from their homes. Hitler provided only the culmination of the process. American white supremacism fits this bill, too.

Ordinary prejudices—for instance, the simple-minded belief that blacks are naturally musical or athletic—are certainly part of the structure of racism. But they are a secondary part. It might be helpful to picture American racism as a tree. Prejudiced attitudes of this sort are part of the tree, organically connected to the root of racism. But they are only the small branches of the tree, which don't hold the tree up or nourish it. Just as we might prune a tree regularly without damaging its health, these prejudiced beliefs can be taken away, but the structure of racism will be essentially unchanged.

Race, Wealth, and Power

The deep, sustaining root of American racism is dominating power exercised for the purpose of economic exploitation. A racist system is one which distributes social rewards—such as status and wealth—on the basis of perceived biological attributes, such as skin color. A racist society, for instance, would be one in which people with skin of one color are disproportionately poor, imprisoned, and underrepresented in the most prestigious professions.

The functioning of such a social order requires a justifying belief system or ideology that holds one group superior to another and defines that difference according to biological characteristics. That's where our ordinary prejudices come in. Such a system also requires mechanisms of social power to enforce that view.

Racism is enforced by the political dominance of the "superior" group. Members of that group control the power of the state and occupy important decision-making posts in major social institutions. These positions are used to maintain the status quo through a system of rewards and punishments. Especially cooperative and pliable members of the oppressed group may be admitted to a sort of honorary membership in the dominant group. Meanwhile, the rebellious and recalcitrant can be suppressed or eliminated by force.

Particularly graphic examples of this can be seen in the history of the British Empire. Throughout their African and Asian dominion, the British created local, Western-educated elites to staff colonial governments, but the British were also absolutely ruthless in their use of armed force whenever a serious threat to British power arose—even to the point of gunning down hundreds of unarmed Indians during Gandhi's nonviolent campaign for independence.

The political control exercised by the dominant group in a racist social order is not a mere ego trip or superiority complex. Power, as common experience tells us, is usually wielded in the service of wealth. The European colonial powers, for instance, established white-ruled societies in Asia and Africa not so that white colonial functionaries could be saluted and served but in order to maintain Europe's free access to the mineral wealth, raw materials, and cheap (or slave) labor of the colonized world.

Our American racial structure is an offspring of that colonial world. It was born to justify the removal of sovereign peoples from their land and the appropriation of human souls as property.

The Minds of White Folk

Power in the service of wealth is the root of a racist system. But that has never been enough to prop up an entire social order. After all, in the racist systems mentioned above, only a very few members of the dominant group actually received the benefits of economic exploitation. For the system to function, something else had to motivate the necessary legions of soldiers, police, teachers, bureaucrats, and ordinary workers. In the colonial societies, including our own, that something has been one form or another of white supremacy.

In a nutshell, white supremacy is the ideology that holds "white" to be the normative condition for "human." This worldview defines and judges all the other groups of people on earth according to their difference from the "white" norm. Asians, Native Americans, and Arabs are all "different" from white people and have, at one time or another, felt the lash of white supremacy. But in the white supremacist hierarchy, African people are the most different of all, and "whiteness" is defined mostly in opposition to the "blackness" of sub-Saharan Africans.

The ideology of white supremacy gives ordinary white people a sense of ownership in the system solely because of the genetic accident of skin color. Some white people might be nearly as poor and powerless as slaves. But white supremacism causes those people to define themselves and their situation in terms of skin color, not wealth and power. It encourages the ordinary white working person to identify with the white people who run the society and join them in supporting and enforcing a social order that oppresses the blacks.

Since it deals in matters of personal identity, white supremacism inevitably reaches into the inner lives of people. It works in the realm of subconscious fears, envies, and resentments, as well as the realm of overt religious belief and political ideology. It forms a shared universe of myths and symbols that allow people bound by one biological characteristic to define themselves as truly human and others as something less.

White supremacism as we know it today is mostly a product of the "Age of Discovery." In the ancient world, people of different skin colors sometimes encountered one another as travelers, trading partners, or antagonists in battle. But we have no evidence that they used skin color as a basis for judgments about character. It was simply one biological trait among others that varied across the geography of the known world. Slavery existed throughout the ancient world, but it was not tied to any notion of race. Slaves were usually people conquered in war, of whatever color or nationality.

In Europe during the Middle Ages, discrimination among people and cultures was made on the basis of religion. Christians often forcibly asserted their superiority over Jews and Muslims, but skin color had nothing to do with these divisions.

All of that changed when the powers of Europe began building global empires. Beginning in 1492, Europeans went out exploring what were, to them, previously unknown reaches of the planet—the Americas, the South Pacific islands, the west coast of Africa, etc. As they went, they encountered what was, to them, a bewildering array of peoples and cultures. The Europeans thought of themselves as occupying the apex of human civilization, so the rest of the world was mainly evaluated and condemned for the ways that it failed to be European, Christian, and "white." This worldview, while sincerely held and sometimes even well-intentioned, had the convenient effect of providing a religious and civilizing rationale for the wholesale seizure of lands, wealth, and peoples in the "discovered" territories.

American white supremacism is a unique product of the encounter between the British and the black Africans. In his landmark work from the 1970s, *White Racism: A Psychohistory*, psychoanalyst Joel Kovel quotes from the *Oxford English Dictionary* the meanings that were given to the word *black* before the sixteenth century, which was before actual black people were much of a factor in the English mind. The "preracial" meanings of blackness "included, 'Deeply stained with dirt; soiled, dirty, foul . . . Having dark or deadly purposes . . . Foul, iniquitous, atrocious, horrible, wicked . . . indicating disgrace, censure, liability punishment, etc.'" In short, Kovel says, blackness represented "the abstract idea of badness itself." It should come as no surprise that in medieval Europe, Satan was depicted as black.

Given this preexisting set of associations, when the English actually saw black people in Africa, there was bound to be psychological trouble. The fact that many black Africans wore very little clothing and seemed not to share Anglo-Saxon inhibitions about sexuality only compounded the trauma. The British identified these things with heathenism. To European eyes, these black people were decadent, pagan, and the color of evil; therefore they must, in fact, be an embodiment of evil. Or, as the

African psychiatrist, Frantz Fanon, put it, "In Europe, the black man is the symbol of Evil. . . . Satan is black; one talks of shadows, when one is dirty one is black—whether one is thinking of physical dirtiness or of moral dirtiness."

These first impressions helped serve to rationalize slavery. The "difference" of black people was so great that the European mind could convince itself that black people were soulless and so could be appropriated as property. And after slavery was instituted, Kovel says, "The fantasies grew in intensity and elaboration until they flowered into the myth of Race."

Psychologists have long recognized a process called "projection," in which people attribute to others around them the very traits that they most hate or fear in themselves. Projection has run rampant in white attitudes toward black people. As Kovel puts it, "Whatever is forbidden and horrifying in human nature, may be designated as black and projected onto a man whose dark skin . . . fit him to receive the symbol." Speaking psychoanalytically, Kovel suggests that white men identified black people with the "id," the hidden, therefore "dark" part of the personality—the repository, in Freudian theory, of repressed desires. So it was that all of the white man's repressed desires, mostly having to do with sex and violence, were projected into the social world as fantasies about black people.

Kovel suggests this is the keystone to what he calls "dominative racism," which came to full expression in the slave societies of the Southern U.S., where black men were attributed with enormous sexual prowess and vast, uncontrollable, violent sexual desires, especially for white women. That particular trick of projection became the fantasy of the black rapist, which was the basis for an untold number of Southern lynchings. That is also why lynchings so often included the castration of the black victim. Kovel convincingly argues that this sexual fear of the black superman has been behind the white racist's need to attack black men's masculinity—for instance, by forcing great shows of subservient behavior, calling them "boy," and, especially during slavery, taking sexual advantage of black women (i.e., doing precisely what he claimed to fear in the black man).

The Southern historical context of captor and captive that nurtured this psychosexual swamp has long since passed, but the myth of the hypersexual, hyperviolent, animalistic black man still lurks just below the surface of contemporary culture. It reared its head most recently during the Hurricane Katrina flood in New Orleans in 2005.

We may recall that during that crisis there were widespread media reports of rapes and murders raging among the predominantly African-American residents of New Orleans emergency shelters. Independent investigations a few months later found no confirmed rapes during the flood and fewer homicides than the city would have experienced in an average week. The horror stories were mostly rumors that spread and gained legitimacy at least in part, because they confirmed what white people were predisposed to believe about black people. Jim Amoss is the white editor of the daily *New Orleans Times Picayune*, a paper which reported some of the false rumors during the flood, and later ran a major piece debunking the horror stories. Amoss acknowledged that the race of the people left behind in New Orleans undoubtedly played a big part in how the Katrina story was reported and perceived.

In Kovel's scheme, the "dominative racist" is obsessed with black people and with exerting power over them. He is complemented by what Kovel calls the "aversive racist," who seeks simply to avoid all contact with black people. Kovel identifies aversive racism with the white North and with more educated and affluent white people. If dominative racism could be seen as growing from the association of blackness with evil and with things hidden in darkness, aversive racism grows from the "preracial" association of blackness with dirt.

A classic expression of aversive racism comes from a

Newsweek survey of racial attitudes in which one white respondent said of black people, "I don't like to touch them. It just makes me squeamish. I know I shouldn't be that way but it still bothers me."

This aversion can be so deep and subtle that, as Kovel points out, the Quakers of the Northeastern U.S.—who were once almost alone among white Americans in seeking justice for black people—still maintained a separate section for black bodies in most of their burial grounds.

Whatever the psychological origins, there is no question that a mythology about black people's dirtiness and smelliness has been a strong undercurrent in white America's racial attitudes. It could be seen in the absurd lengths to which segregation laws went to keep black and white people from sitting next to each other or using any of the same public facilities. Even in the North, blacks were commonly banned from many hotels and restaurants.

More recently, aversive racism is one subtle and usually unconscious factor behind white flight from neighborhoods and school systems. Researchers have noted that today white flight doesn't occur at the first sight of black people in an area. If the black people are on the same economic level as the whites, the first breeching of the color barrier usually brings smiling toasts to "diversity." Instead, white flight kicks in when the percentage of black people in a neighborhood reaches a level at which whites begin to feel "crowded" by them or feel that the black people are too close. There's no magic number for this "feeling," but researchers did recently survey random groups of black and white homeowners as to what they thought constituted an appropriate level of racial integration for a neighborhood. The blacks thought the optimal level of integration would be a black population of 35 to 50 percent. The whites thought the black population should be more like 8 percent. Blacks make up about 13 percent of the total U.S. population, and comprise a much higher percentage than that in most Southern states and in the larger Northern cities. So these survey results could be extrapolated to suggest that many white people think there are simply too many African-Americans in "their" country.

The fantasies and myths of white racism are, of course, not limited to the minds of white folks. It is inevitable that, after three hundred years of constant reinforcement, many of these notions would be internalized by black people too. In fact, the destruction of black people's self-image and regard for their own people may be white racism's greatest crime. Kovel puts it this way:

> Whites have created the institutions by which black people are forced to live, and which force them to live in a certain way, almost invariably so as to foster that constellation of unworthy traits . . . dirty, feckless, lazy, irrational. . . . The accumulation of negative images forced upon blacks in America amounted to presenting them with one massive and destructive choice: either to hate one's self, as the culture so systematically demanded, or to have no self at all, to be nothing.

For more than three hundred years, black people in America have been targets for the projection of white people's shameful secret desires, the objects of many white people's power- and pleasure-seeking, and the despised "untouchables" of our caste system. They've been labeled as violent and promiscuous, mentally inferior, and physically strong. In a situation where white people have held almost all the power, these myths, images, and projections have become so deeply rooted that they have even shaped some of our reality.

As American as Apple Pie

American racism is now part of our national heritage—like baseball and the Fourth of July. It grows out of our particular historical experience, and it distinguishes us from other nations and cultures. It might be useful to make an analogy between American racism and American individualism. For two hundred years observers have noted that Americans, of all classes and ethnic groups, are more individualistic than people of other nations. In a world where most people revere tradition and playing by the rules, we Americans assume a God-given right to drive our own cars, pursue our own dreams, and start over in the next town if our dreams turn sour.

There are many explanations for this uniquely American characteristic. One is our mostly self-selected immigrant population of people who chose to abandon their old homes and family ties and strike out on their own. Many Americans were formed by the experience of survival on the vast frontier, where neighbors were few and distant and self-reliance was a primary virtue. Whatever its causes, at this point individualism is so ingrained in our character that we don't even recognize it. It is, however, stunningly obvious to visitors from more traditional and communal cultures, where the odds of survival reward cooperation and group-thinking.

We Americans are all individualists, but when a worldview is that universal and inherited, it's almost meaningless to call any one American an "individualist." We only become individualists when we become aware of the choice between individual and group interests and choose to act as if our individual freedom and happiness are more important than the groups to which we belong. And we only begin to overcome individualism after we have made a conscious choice to reorient our moral lives away from self-seeking at every level.

The parallel to racism is almost exact. Every white American participates in racism. We can't help it. We are born into a society that, for more than two-thirds of its history, granted citizenship and opportunity to almost all white people while holding people of African descent as property and decimating the native population. That pattern of distributing power and status on the basis of skin color runs down to the deepest roots of our country. That's how America accumulated its wealth and capital. The color distinction was even enshrined in our Constitution, where slaves were counted as three-fifths of a person. Without some moral intervention, a white American will breathe in the assumptions of white supremacy and black inferiority almost from birth. Wave after wave of immigrants have absorbed it as part of their Americanization. Like individualism, it is simply "in the air."

We white Americans begin life mired in complicity with racism. It's meaningless to call us "racists" until we choose to consciously act on the idea that white skin confers superiority. Still, we can't escape our participation in structural racism until we make a fundamental choice to reorient all of our thinking and acting. Making that choice against racism requires rooting ourselves intellectually in an understanding of the historic and economic forces that have caused racism and spiritually in the new reality of the kingdom of God.

Crawling out of the psychosocial morass of white supremacy will not be simple. The process has begun in the past fifty years, but it will take generations. It begins every time we name a myth for what it is and insist on the truth that what we call "races" are mere genetic accidents.

But for racial progress to continue, psychological healing and liberation will have to be accompanied by attention to the material circumstances of political power and economic exploitation. As we will see, the one has fed the other since the 1600s, and they still do.

Chapter 3

The Original Wedge Issue

American racism began to take living shape in the 1600s in the Virginia colony. By the end of that century, the features of white supremacy as we would come to know it were already recognizable. But it didn't start that way, and it didn't have to end that way.

Most of us know, at most, three things about the Virginia colony: the founding date of Jamestown (1607), the Pocahontas story, and the date of the arrival of the first Africans (1619). That is usually given as the beginning point of slavery in the future U.S. In 1619, Africans were already enslaved in the Spanish, Portuguese, and Dutch colonies of the New World. In fact, those first Africans to arrive in Virginia were purchased off a Dutch ship that had stopped in Jamestown en route from the Caribbean to New Amsterdam (what is now New York). With this background, we generally presume that the institution of African slavery for life arrived in Virginia with them, fully formed.

The truth is more complex and ambiguous. It was not written in the sky that Africans in America would occupy a special category of subhuman servitude. When the Africans arrived in Virginia, they took their places in a society with varying degrees and conditions of servitude—none of them based on color. But by the end of the seventeenth century, Virginians of African descent did occupy a separate category in which dark skin color was identified with lifelong slavery. To understand white supremacy in America, we have to understand how that happened. It was during that century that skin color, rather than religion or economic class, started to become the main dividing line in American society.

At first in the Virginia colony, people of different colors acted according to their economic interests as servants and masters. Of the white people doing physical labor in the Virginia colony in 1619, almost none were free. Tobacco was the colony's main crop. Tobacco production requires a lot of hard manual work, and volunteers to do it were in short supply. So most ordinary Virginians arrived from the British Isles as indentured servants. They served a term in bondage (usually seven years) and were set free at the end. These people were shipped out of British debtors' prisons or sold themselves in return for passage to the New World. The term of bondage was often extended if an indentured servant violated an ever-growing list of rules in the colony's "servant code," but the presumption of both master and servant was that someday the servant would go free.

Lifelong slavery existed in the Virginia colony before the Africans arrived, but it was reserved for non-Christians or "heathens." Before 1619, this applied exclusively to the native Indians. Afterward, it also applied to some Africans. But in the 1600s, even slavery for life was not as harsh an institution as it would become in Virginia. Slaves could own, buy, and sell livestock. They could work for wages and use the proceeds to buy their freedom. One 1646 Virginia court case required a slave's permission before he could be sold.

In the early days, some African slaves were freed when they converted to Christianity. Some other Africans came into Virginia as indentured servants under the same terms as their British, Scottish, or Irish counterparts, and some of them became free at the end of their terms. Once Africans were free, they became full members of the community. They owned property and even servants. There are recorded cases of intermarriage between blacks and whites. Undoubtedly, there was racial prejudice and private discrimination in the early days of the Virginia colony, but there was no separate, race-based legal status for blacks. Yet by 1691, Virginia had passed a law against interracial marriage, a clear indication that the status of blacks had changed for the worse.

Drawing the Color Line

What happened in the last half of the seventeenth century to so radically and quickly change the legal status of blacks? The explanation lies in the servants' revolts that shook the Virginia colony in the 1660s and 1670s. By the 1660s, the Virginia colony was developing a major servant problem—what to do with them once they were free. The colonial legislature made the "servant code" stricter to help masters lengthen the terms of servitude. This angered many servants, but it didn't solve the systematic problem. Even the most unruly and unlucky servant would eventually be freed. The freed servants couldn't be shipped back to England. They weren't wanted there. That's why they'd come to Virginia in the first place. So they were turned loose, without resources or prospects, and, not surprisingly, they caused trouble.

The freed servants wanted land, but increasingly the land along the coastal plain was already claimed. When former servants moved on to Indian lands to the West, they provoked Indian attacks on both themselves and long-established settlers. Then the freedmen demanded that British soldiers come to protect their inland settlements from the Indians. But in those days the British army was busy with a revolution and a civil war back home.

As the number of servants grew with the passing years, so did the problems and so did their discontent. In 1663, a group of servants in Gloucester County began meeting at Mr. Knight's tavern, a place frequented by whites and blacks of the laboring class. They began complaining about their plight—especially about the ever-lengthening terms of service for the slightest infractions of the servant code. The men ended up planning definitive action. Nine of the men entered an agreement to collect weapons and recruit others with the aim of launching a revolt. They planned to meet at a designated spot on September 13, 1663, and begin marching across the countryside to Jamestown. They expected to seize more weapons as they went and recruit additional soldiers from the plantation servants and slaves. Eventually they planned to besiege the governor in Jamestown and demand freedom for all servants and slaves.

The plot was stopped by an informer. But its seriousness can be judged from the reaction of the Virginia legislature. The informer was rewarded with 5,000 pounds of tobacco. The four chief leaders of the planned revolt were executed. The House of Burgesses, a legislative body dominated by the landed elite, des-ignated September 13 as an annual day of thanksgiving that the revolt had been averted.

But the feared revolt wasn't averted; it was only postponed. It arrived in 1676, when a young planter named Nathaniel Bacon took up the cause of the former servants who had taken over inland land claims. At first, their demand was for stronger action against the native Indians. Then Bacon and the small freeholders took up arms against the Indians themselves. But from the begin-ning, mixed in with the small farmers' anti-Indian sentiments was real and righteous anger at the growing inequality and cor-ruption of the colonial social order.

As Bacon put it, "The poverty of the country is such that all the power and sway is got into the hands of the rich who . . . hav-ing the common people in their debt have always curbed and oppressed them." On another occasion, Bacon called the colony's "great men in authority" a collection of "sponges [who] have sucked up the public treasures."

When no relief or reform was forthcoming from the rulers of the colony, Bacon left some of his men to continue fighting the Indians in the West while he led another armed group in a march on Jamestown. There Bacon's army ousted the governor and temporarily seized control of the colony. The governor counterattacked with 1,000 British troops, and Bacon called all his men in from the frontier to focus on the fight with Virginia's ruling elite. Needing more troops to counter the British, Bacon proclaimed freedom for all slaves and servants who joined his army. The governor had earlier tried this tactic, but no bondsmen had heeded the call. But hundreds of servants and slaves from throughout the colony flocked to Bacon's cause and made it their own.

For several weeks during the summer of 1676, a biracial army of indentured servants, slaves, and poor white farmers marched through the Tidewater section of Virginia, looting the homes of the wealthy planters and recruiting plantation slaves and servants to join the fight. A battle that had begun around the narrow interests of a small section of what we would call the "lower middle class" had turned into a revolutionary movement to abolish all forms of forced labor and unearned privilege. For a moment, it seemed possible that Virginia might be the birthplace of the world's first multiracial cooperative commonwealth.

Then the tide turned. Bacon got sick and died, but the leaderless army of the poor fought on. The British sent reinforcements and heavier weaponry. Finally a British gunship sailed up the York River for a final assault on the movement's garrison. Four hundred men were there. Most of them surrendered for fear of the cannon fire and under false promises of freedom. A small group of eighty blacks and twenty whites fought on until they ran out of ammunition.

Bacon's Rebellion represented the turning point in the evolution of race-based slavery and the ideology of white supremacy that came with it. The planters realized that indentured servants would not provide the stable, secure supply of cheap labor that they needed. Since earlier attempts to enslave the Indians had failed, that left the African slave trade as the only alternative. Planters began to import more black African slaves, and their legislature passed the antimiscegenation law. Africans were consigned to an inferior "other" category based not on religion, or even condition of servitude, but purely on skin color.

At the same time, the colony took measures to improve the lot of freed white servants. In 1705, a new law guaranteed all freed servants severance pay in the form of ten bushels of corn, thirty shillings in cash, a gun, and fifty acres of land. So the commonality of interest between lower-class whites and blacks was broken. They were divided and separated along racial lines. The poor whites were given material incentives to identify with the "big men" of the colony as their allies and protectors against the blacks. And so it has remained in America for three hundred years.

In his concerts in the 1980s, singer-songwriter Bruce Springsteen would sometimes talk about the petty trappings of middle-class American consumerism as a sort of consolation prize for the loss of genuine democracy. He half-joked that all of it—the suburban houses, the second and third cars, the boats, the home entertainment systems—was a "booby prize," a poor substitute for real power and real equality. Especially for lower-income white people, the privilege of "whiteness"—simply being "better" than the blacks—has been chief among those booby prizes. The white indentured servants of Virginia were the first Americans to be offered it, and they eagerly took it. The alternative, after all, had been crushed beneath a hail of cannonballs.

In the early twenty-first century, we've heard a lot about "wedge issues" in American politics. These are the social and cultural issues—such as abortion, gay rights, and gun control—that the Republican Party has used to separate white working-class Americans from their former allegiance to the Democrats. It is an effective strategy, but it is not a new one. Race was the original wedge issue in America, and its successful use dates back to the late 1600s.

The Republic of Slavery

During the eighteenth and nineteenth centuries, the institution of race-based slavery for life continued to evolve in the colonies and new American nation. Contrary to our usual notions of human progress, the slave system in America actually grew more brutal and inhumane as the years wore on. At the same time the doctrines of white supremacy upon which the slave system depended became more and more deeply rooted and intrinsic to the character of the young country.

In the late 1700s, at the time of the American founding, the slave system had become less profitable. At the Constitutional Convention in 1787, there was serious talk of its abolition, and even Southern defenders of slavery assumed that the institution would evolve out of existence within a few decades. But that changed with the invention of the mechanical cotton gin, which made large-scale cultivation of cotton—another labor-intensive cash crop—viable throughout the Deep South states. This development resulted in massive growth of the enslaved population. In *A People's History of the United States*, Howard Zinn reports that in 1790, there were about 500,000 slaves in the U.S. By 1860, there were four million. Stricter laws and harsher practices were developed to control the larger slave workforce. Southern landowners' commitment to the economics of slavery and their defense of it in national politics also hardened in the early 1800s, ensuring that the racial politics of slavery would come to dominate the politics of the entire nation, even in states where slavery had been abolished and where few black people lived. This is when the issue of race moved to the center of America's national politics and stayed there for the next 150 years.

In the first half of the nineteenth century, whites were a minority in much of the Deep South. They lived surrounded by and dependent upon other human beings over whom they claimed absolute power and ownership. And they lived with a secret, guilty terror that those other human beings might be just like them: they might love their families, and they might wish to be free.

The conditions of plantation slavery made organized rebellions difficult, but they did happen. In 1822, Denmark Vesey, a free black man in Charleston, South Carolina, led a massive conspiracy that aimed to burn that city (then America's sixth largest) to the ground. An informer betrayed Vesey's rebellion, but by the time the authorities discovered the plot, slaves had already assembled an arsenal of 550 homemade weapons, suggesting that hundreds, perhaps thousands, of slaves were involved in the plan. Vesey and thirty-five other rebels were tried and hanged. Afterward court records of the trial were destroyed to keep blacks in the future from learning of and drawing inspiration from the rebellion plot.

In 1831, back in the Tidewater section of Virginia, the uprising that Southern whites had feared finally occurred. A slave preacher named Nat Turner led seventy of his fellow slaves on a bloody march through Southampton County. They murdered at least fifty-five white men, women, and children before they ran out of ammunition and were captured. Turner and eighteen others were hanged.

Zinn tells us that at the time of the Turner Rebellion, Virginia had a total population of about 1.2 million, and an armed, organized militia force of 101,000. America had no foreign enemies during those years. This garrison state was maintained solely to control the enslaved population, but it still couldn't save the lives of Turner's fifty-five victims. The Turner Rebellion, like Bacon's 155 years before, presented white Virginians—and all white Southerners—with an historic choice. They could acknowledge the futility of trying to hold other human beings in absolute bondage and prepare to dismantle the slave system, or they could dig in and do whatever was necessary to protect themselves and their wealth. Most chose the latter course. Locally, slave owners became more relentless in controlling and disciplining their slaves, and nationally they campaigned to have slavery made a permanent feature of American life by extending it to new territories in the West.

By this time, Southern slave owners had become so committed to a way of life based on human bondage that few could any longer imagine an alternative. But they were only able to persist in this course because the ideas of white supremacy and black inferiority had also become broadly accepted in the North. Slavery may have come about because it was very profitable and convenient for a few, very powerful people. But those people were still human beings, with souls and emotions. In order to quiet their consciences and face their children, they had to tell themselves some story in which the absolute subjugation of black people made sense.

The Invention of "Races"

This "story" became the ideology of white supremacy. It came in versions both scientific and religious, and in the1800s, it became widely accepted throughout the United States. The pseudo-science of nineteenth-century racism divided human beings into three general categories or "races": the Caucasoid (white), Mongoloid (Asian), and Negroid (African)—with dozens of shades of brown in between. By the simple expedient of declaring "white" physical characteristics the normative human ones, these early anthropologists defined whites as the apex of creation, or later, evolution. Asians were a slightly degraded form of white people. Africans were defined as barely human. In this view, blacks were plainly created or adapted for the sole purpose of hard labor in the hot sun.

One religious variant of this racialist theory held that the black skin of Africans was in fact the visible sign placed upon Noah's son, Ham, who was cursed with a life of eternal servitude. The more respectable religious versions of white supremacy held that slavery was the means God had chosen to bring the pagan Africans into the knowledge of Christianity and Western civilization. This view was always buttressed by exhaustive references to the existence of slavery in biblical times and the failure of the Jewish law, the prophets, Jesus, or the New Testament church to condemn it. Paul's counsel to Philemon to be content in his condition of servitude was especially useful in this regard.

Attempts to justify slavery from the Bible ignored the fact that slavery in biblical times was not so harsh and permanent as it was in nineteenth-century America, nor was it based on "race." In fact, there is no evidence that people in biblical times attributed any significance to differences of skin color.

The doctrines of white racial supremacy, as they were known in nineteenth century America and as they have survived to this day, are creations of the modern world. They came about mainly as a result of the British empire's project of exploring, conquering, and subduing the nonwhite world. The slave trade was a part of this imperial undertaking, and it brought both African people and the doctrine of their inferiority to American shores. Here white supremacy took on a life of its own.

But it is crucial to recognize that white racism is not a "natural" phenomenon. Yes, prejudice against outsiders, and even scapegoating of them, does seem to be part of human nature. But the systematic dehumanization of an entire people solely on the basis of certain physical traits is not natural. It had to be learned and taught.

At the beginning of the American experiment in the 1600s, when black and white people were first thrust together, they acted naturally. They intermarried, and they acted cooperatively around common interests. Their separation into "races" came about to serve the economic interests of the wealthy classes in the Southern colonies. It had to be engineered by a system of rewards and punishments and justified by scientific and religious theories. In the process of constructing a system around the acceptance of race-based slavery, most white Americans came to betray the ideals of their own democratic revolution, the spirit of their own religion, and in the end, their own humanity. Only in the past fifty years—since the start of the modern civil rights movement—has any serious effort been made to reverse that betrayal.

A Workable Alliance?

At the end of the Civil War, America had a chance to begin again. Slavery was abolished. The power of the Southern planters was broken, and the region was a blank slate upon which a new chapter in race relations could be written. Again, as they had in 1676, democratic ideals and economic enterprise would come into conflict.

As the war was ending, a great debate had already begun over postwar Reconstruction policy. Despite being interrupted and distorted by the assassination of President Lincoln, this debate proceeded on two levels. The one we usually hear about in our history books was between Democrats and Republicans over how harshly to treat the white rebels of the South. But an equally important debate took place within the Republican Party over what kind of economy and society would be created in the occupied South.

The Republican Party had begun its life in 1854 as the party of antislavery small farmers, workers, and tradespeople in the West and Midwest (what had been the "Free Soil" movement). These folk were opposed to slavery both because of their revivalist

Christianity and because they couldn't compete with crops grown or goods produced by slave labor. This agrarian and working-class base was joined in the new party by the Northeastern abolitionists who represented a moral constituency against slavery. When the Republican Party came to power and led the nation into war, it also became the political home of America's emerging industrial capitalists and financiers. The captains of industry had no moral interest one way or another in slavery, but they supported the Republicans and their war against the Southern Confederacy, if only for all the production of cannons, rifles, wagons, and ships a war required.

Northern capitalists were also ready to see slavery end. They were against slavery for the same reasons that their predecessors in England had abolished the feudal way of life in the countryside and their contemporaries in Russia were against serfdom. These were all vestiges of the precapitalist, agrarian way of life, and they had to be removed to make way for free markets, including a free market in labor.

While the Civil War was on, these diverging moral and economic interests could coexist peacefully under the Republican tent. But when the war was over, the differences surfaced. Many of the old Free Soilers and abolitionists, now called Radical Republicans, proposed to break up the Southern plantations. They saw that without resources or education, African-Americans in the South would be just as vulnerable to exploitation after slavery as they had been during it. If the plantation system and the power of the plantation owners remained intact, slavery—with all its moral and economic evils—would continue under another name. These Republicans called for the federal government to seize plantation lands and redistribute them to the landless poor—black and white alike.

If this course had been taken, all of America's racial history since could have been different. African-American historian Barbara Fields has written that:

A [Reconstruction] program combining land redistribution with debtors' relief might have permitted both freedmen and yeomen whites to live, for a time, in the essentially self-sufficient peasant manner that both groups seem to have preferred. . . . With a sounder material basis for political cooperation and with their grievances more in phase with each other, the yeomen and the freedmen might have been able to build a workable alliance. . . . Prejudice would no doubt have remained . . . [but] . . . set in a context which allowed for a less stunted and impoverished existence for both groups, and which provided a basis for political cooperation, it might have taken a less virulent and overwhelming form.

But as it actually happened, Reconstruction was not concerned with either racial equality or righting the wrongs of the past. It did involve the necessity of extending citizenship rights to the former slaves, but the real goal, Fields says, was to establish "national unification on the basis of a system of formally free labor mediated through the market." This meant that both the freed slaves and the white subsistence farmers (the "yeoman" class) had to be converted into wage laborers on the plantations producing raw materials and in the mills, mines, and factories of the "New South" that Southern businessmen were already proclaiming.

According to Fields, the North lost interest in the freed slaves when the freedmen did not pan out as workers in the capitalist scheme. In documents from the period, she reports finding repeated Northern "complaints about undependable work habits." She says those same complaints also occurred "in every part of the world, whenever an employer class . . . has tried to induce men and women unbroken to market discipline to work in exchange for a wage. The planters, indeed, made the same complaints about the people whom they contemptuously labeled crackers [or] rednecks."

On the capitalists' behalf, Fields admits that Northern investors sincerely believed that "in offering the freedmen the chance to become free wage laborers, they were offering them a wonderful boon. But the freedmen knew what they wanted. . . . They wanted their own land, and the right to farm it as they chose. . . . Most found bizarre the white folks' preoccupation with growing things [e.g. cotton] that no one could eat."

Still, without a shred of official encouragement, a "workable alliance" between freed slaves and poor whites did briefly emerge in the postwar South. From 1865 to 1876, the states of the Confederacy were under Federal occupation. During these years the Thirteenth, Fourteenth and Fifteenth Amendments were passed, abolishing slavery and granting full citizenship rights to the former slaves. In addition, Congress passed a number of laws guaranteeing the basic civil rights of African-Americans, and the Freedmen's Bureau was established to try to meet the needs of the former slaves. Under Federal rule, blacks were allowed to vote and run for office, and many were elected as state legislators, congressmen, senators, sheriffs and mayors all over the Deep South. During these years, the first public schools were instituted in the South and other public improvements were made.

Federal troops were withdrawn in 1877, and fifteen years of social, political, and racial ferment and struggle began. In that very same year, the U.S. experienced a major economic depression. In the cities, factories closed and workers went hungry. In rural America—North and South—thousands of farmers lost their land, and desperation swept the countryside.

That year in Texas a group of farmers formed the first Farmers Alliance. By 1886, 100,000 farmers had joined in 2,000 Alliance chapters. They formed buyers' and sellers' cooperatives which helped farmers negotiate lower prices for their supplies and higher prices for their produce. Black farmers organized into a parallel "Colored Alliance." An editorial in an Alabama Alliance newspaper read, "The white and colored alliance are united in their war against the trusts, and in promotion of the doctrine that farmers should establish cooperative stores and manufactures . . . and have a hand in everything . . . that concerns them as citizens." A leader of the Florida Colored Alliance said, "We are aware of the fact that the laboring colored man's interests and the laboring white man's interests are one and the same."

The movement spread rapidly across the South and Midwest. By 1889, there was a National Farmers Alliance with at least 400,000 active members. They began to see the need for governmental changes—regulation of railroad rates, loosening of fiscal policy—if their program was to succeed, but neither of the major political parties was interested in reform, so in 1890 the Alliance spawned the People's Party (or Populist Party).

The move into electoral politics brought the issue of Southern interracial cooperation to the forefront. Black people were still voting in much of the South, so to succeed, the People's Party had to draw some black Southern voters away from the Republicans—the party of Emancipation. This necessity pushed Southern populists ever closer to a true alliance of equals. In Texas, two blacks were elected to the new party's executive committee. "They are in the ditch just like we are," said a white populist leader. In North Carolina, blacks were elected to local offices on the Peoples' Party ticket, with white support. In Georgia, where twenty-four black delegates attended the Peoples' Party convention, party leader, Tom Watson, urged interracial unity. "You are kept apart," he said, "so that you may be separately fleeced of your earnings. You are made to hate each other because upon that hatred is rested the keystone of the arch of financial despotism which enslaves you both."

The ghosts of Bacon's army were stirring again. As Southern historian C. Vann Woodward put it in *The Strange Career of Jim Crow*, "Never before or since have the two races in the South come so close together as they did during the Populist struggle."

Then it all ended. "Power concedes nothing without a struggle," the abolitionist ex-slave Frederick Douglass wrote. And the power of the Southern white ruling class was now aroused as it had not been since the Civil War. In a few places, Klan or Klan-like groups attacked interracial populist gatherings. "Bourbon Democrats," representing the planter class and Democratic courthouse machines, still controlled most of the state legislatures in the South. They adopted new state constitutions and passed laws designed to disenfranchise black and poor white voters, make interracial organizing difficult, and erect a wall of separation between the two races that had been moving closer together. The 1890s was the time when the poll tax and literacy test became requirements for voting in the South. It was also the time when "Jim Crow" laws were passed that required segregation of the races in almost every imaginable public context. "White" and "Colored" signs went up all over the South, and the possibility of a "workable alliance" between black and white was lost for decades to come.

The White American Century

At the end of the nineteenth century, as America's wealth and power grew, so did the conviction of most white citizens that this was and should be "a white man's country." White supremacy was becoming the unifying ideology for a nation that now spanned the North American continent. Throughout the last half of the nineteenth century, the violent removal of the native nations from their lands in the West proceeded efficiently. By any means necessary, soldiers cleared the way for the railroads and opened land for the steady stream of European immigrants still coming to America. In 1890, as Jim Crow was coming to the South, the last openly rebellious Indians were slaughtered at Wounded Knee, South Dakota.

Chinese immigrants had been imported to build the western end of the transcontinental railroad. When that job was finished, they came under violent attack by whites who viewed them as competing for jobs. Western novelist Bret Harte wrote a newspaper obituary for a Chinese man named Wan Lee which read, "Dead, my revered friends, dead. Stoned to death in the streets of San Francisco . . . by a mob of half-grown boys and Christian school children." In Rock Springs, Wyoming, in 1885, whites staged an unprovoked attack on a group of Chinese miners and killed twenty-eight of them.

At its dawn, the twentieth century was hailed as "the American Century." It began with America exerting its power on the world stage by seizing Cuban and Filipino colonies from Spain and taking a decisive role in Europe's First World War. The next move of the American century was to codify the country's "white" identity. After decades of an open-door policy, in 1920, Congress passed a new law that set immigration quotas for every country on earth. No African country could send more than one hundred people, nor could China or Palestine. But the law set a quota of 34,007 for immigrants from England, 51,227 for Germany and 28,567 for Ireland.

Chapter 4

What Did White Christians Do?

Only one other influence on American life has been as pervasive and enduring as race, and that is Christianity. While debates about the place of religion in politics are heated today, contemporary commentators tend to—wrongly—date the beginning of the controversy to the late 1970s and the intense religious backlash against legalized abortion. The fact is that religion has been part of American politics at least since the landing of the Puritans at Plymouth.

The United States of America was founded as the world's first secular republic, but that did not lead to a withering of religion in American life. Instead, it freed the churches to display unprecedented creativity as they competed for members and social influence. As a result, conflicting visions about the central question of race have often been worked out in the terminology of Christian theology and in the practice of the Christian churches.

In the early days of English colonization in the Americas, most Christians and their churches accepted slavery as part of the natural order of things. Clergy and laypeople alike often pointed out that slavery existed in the time of the Jewish prophets, Jesus Christ, and the early church, yet nowhere in Scripture is the institution explicitly condemned. Christians often pointed to the New Testament epistles of Paul and Peter in which slaves are advised to be obedient and accepting. In addition, many English, and later

American, Christians adhered to an interpretation of Genesis 9 and 10 which held that contemporary Africans were descended from Ham, the son of Noah who was cursed and condemned to be a servant.

In fact, Christian acceptance of slavery in the English colonies was so complete several bishops of the Church of England were large slave-owners; and, as the BBC has reported, the Church itself, through its "Society for the Propagation of the Gospel in Foreign Parts," owned hundreds of slaves on a Barbados plantation. As a contemporary Anglican clergyman has recounted, the Church had its slaves branded with "the word 'society' ... on their backs with a red-hot iron" as an emblem of ownership.

At the same time, Christian opposition to slavery was present almost from the beginning of the African trade. It started with the Quakers, who banned slave traders from their membership in 1761, and spread to the new Methodist movement led by John Wesley and to sympathetic evangelicals within the Church of England. In 1833, these forces succeeded in banning slavery in British-ruled territories.

Christian opposition to slavery was also growing in the first years of the American republic. The revolution and the founding of the new nation were followed almost immediately by one of the most remarkable religious revivals in all of history—the Second Great Awakening. (The First Awakening had swept New England several decades before.) During this time, Protestant evangelists traveled the frontier and drew tens of thousands of people to camp meetings that went on for several days or even weeks. The revivals left in their wake hundreds of new evangelical Protestant congregations across what are now the states of the South and Midwest.

The leaders and converts of the Second Great Awakening showed zeal for evangelism and for moral reform—of the individual and the society. The first movements to limit the sale of alcohol emerged from the Second Great Awakening, and so did a mainstream white constituency against slavery. In the beginning, the revivals of the Second Great Awakening were racially mixed—even in the South. And the ethic of the new evangelicalism tended to be egalitarian. The African was seen as a child of God on an equal spiritual footing with whites, and the institution of slavery was seen as an offense against God himself.

Charles Finney, the most prominent American revivalist preacher of the early nineteenth century, saw Christian support for slavery as one of the chief obstacles to spiritual revival in his time. "One of the reasons," Finney wrote, "for the low state of religion at the present time is that many Churches have taken the wrong side on the subject of slavery, have suffered prejudice to prevail over principle, and have feared to call this abomination by its true name."

Meanwhile, in the Northeast, the Quakers, with their base in Pennsylvania had always represented a solid antislavery constituency. From the earliest colonial days, they raised a Christian voice of conscience against all overt racism. To the Quakers, Christ's command to love our neighbor applied equally to Europeans, Africans, and Native Americans. Further up the Atlantic coast, at the dawn of the nineteenth century, New England Puritans had been evolving into more liberal Congregationalists, and some Congregationalists were evolving into free-thinking Unitarians. In New England, the liberal churches competed with evangelicals by promoting revivals of personal piety and strengthening their commitment to social reform. All of these liberal religious groups of the Northeast were united in a moral passion for the abolition of slavery.

Nowhere, it seemed, did the American marketplace of religion offer any justification for slavery. At the time of the Second Great Awakening (the turn from the eighteenth to nineteenth centuries), the main argument for slavery was simply that the economies of the Southern states still depended upon it. But, at that time, slave-based plantations were becoming less profitable with each passing year. It was easy to imagine that in the nineteenth century, slavery in the new nation would simply fade away from a combination of moral disapproval and economic inefficiency.

Degrees of Abolitionism

In the early 1800s, however, there was no consensus among anti-slavery Christians about how to eliminate the institution. On the deeper question of race, there was very little support in any region or denomination for incorporating African-Americans as fully equal partners in building a new nation.

Not every antislavery Christian was an abolitionist. Many, perhaps most, believed that Christians should oppose slavery by moral persuasion and evangelism. If enough individual slave owners became true Christians, this line of reasoning insisted, then the slavery problem would solve itself. Only a minority of antislavery evangelicals in the heartland would have endorsed using the power of government to force slaveholders to relinquish their human property.

In the East, there was a significant body of abolitionist Christians. They staffed the Underground Railroad to help slaves escape bondage; they supported a network of abolitionist newspapers; and they elected abolitionist congressmen who kept the moral question of slavery before the nation. Most abolitionists were prepared to have the federal government assert its power to end slavery. But even among abolitionists there was no consensus about what would come next.

Few abolitionists were prepared to argue for the full social and political equality of African-Americans, much less actually to live on that basis. Joel Kovel's "aversive racism" had already made great inroads into the Northern liberal psyche. Some abolitionists argued that freed Africans should be repatriated to West Africa. A pilot repatriation project was begun in the early 1800s and resulted in the founding of the nation of Liberia, with its capital, Monrovia, named for U.S. President James Monroe.

The prevailing racial attitudes in the liberal North can be inferred from the language of an 1843 fundraising appeal for a black children's school in Philadelphia. The anonymous author wrote:

> We know there is a feeling of hostility and prejudice existing against this people, and a wish is often expressed by many, that they could be removed from amongst us. It might be desirable to have them away, but there are many things desirable which are not practicable. They are here, and are likely to remain here.... For your own sake then, contribute to enlighten a population which you cannot remove from among you, that the burden of this disagreeable contact may be rendered as light as possible.

At no time in the nineteenth century were there more than a very few white visionaries who could imagine that Africans might take their place alongside Europeans as equal partners in building American democracy. Even for many of the most well-meaning and conscientious people, white supremacy had become so deeply rooted that the idea of a racially mixed society was simply unthinkable.

So, during the fervor of the Second Great Awakening, Christian reformers failed to unite around a political program that would actually eliminate the evil of race-based slavery. As we've seen, a couple of decades later—due to the mechanization of cotton production and the Nat Turner Rebellion—the economic and political winds began to change, and much of the general moral sentiment against slavery was dissipated. In the South, questioning the institution became unthinkable.

During the period of the nineteenth century when the Protestant churches struggled over slavery, American Catholics were a relatively powerless minority, concerned mainly with assimilating into the American mainstream. While the Vatican issued documents condemning the slave trade, U.S. Catholic Church leaders tended to see slavery as a political issue beyond their field of responsibility. It can rightly be said that the U.S. Catholic hierarchy, and most American Catholics, supported the continuation of slavery, if only through their silence. *The National Catholic Reporter* notes that the late Catholic historian Msgr. John Tracy Ellis called this collaboration in the evil of slavery "the greatest blot" on the record of the American Catholic Church.

Silence about slavery was also found among many American Protestants. In theology and practice, revivalist Protestant Christianity had always centered on the conversion and sanctification of individuals—changing one heart at a time. That individualism provided white Southern evangelicals with the cover they needed. Most of them retreated (permanently) behind the proposition that the gospel was only relevant to the salvation of individual souls in the next life and had nothing whatever to say about the arrangement of wealth and power in this one.

In the rest of the country, many mainstream evangelicals, while still seeing the elimination of slavery as a goal of Christian reform, also were discouraged by the practical obstacles to its achievement. In the middle decades of the nineteenth century, as the political crisis over slavery deepened, the voice of Christian abolitionists (white and black) was still heard throughout the Northern states. But the abolitionists comprised only a prophetic minority, and a small one at that, of American Protestant Christians.

After the Civil War, the abolitionist strand in American Protestantism continued its engagement with social issues and evolved into the "social gospel" movement. These Christians took on the cause of women's suffrage, the exploitation of workers in America's Industrial Revolution, and the horrifying conditions in early twentieth-century slums. The differences between social gospel Christians and evangelicals who promoted a gospel of individual salvation and personal piety sharpened and deepened and resulted in a historic split in American society—a precursor to the twenty-first century "culture wars."

Chapter 5

A Third Great Awakening

After the failure of the populist rebellion in the 1880s, the racist status quo reasserted itself in the South, where the vast majority of African-Americans continued to live. In every state of the old Confederacy, new post-Reconstruction constitutions enshrined racial segregation with the force of law and effectively deprived black people of the right to vote. These were popularly known as the "Jim Crow" constitutions (a nickname for segregation derived from the name of a common minstrel show character). Meanwhile, the sharecropping system was instituted as a replacement for slavery in working the large Southern plantations.

Under slavery, a Southern planter maintained a small army of laborers to work his large land area under the watchful eye of an overseer. Under sharecropping, each black family (and many poor white ones) was given responsibility for working a small portion of the plantation land. The family was provided with a small house, a mule, and the necessary tools, seed, and supplies—all charged (often at grossly inflated prices) as an advance payment against the harvest. At harvest time, the landowner took half the crop and the sharecropper took half. The sharecropper then had to pay all of his year's expenses out of his share. If he couldn't repay the total, he began the next year in debt.

Sharecropping resulted in a form of debt slavery that insured the stability of the work force almost as efficiently as chattel slavery had. If an indebted family tried to leave a plantation, they weren't exercising their human rights—they were trying to escape their legal obligations to the landowner. At best, sharecropping was a bad system. At its worst, unscrupulous landowners could use it to trick illiterate people out of their freedom and livelihood.

Southern blacks were also kept in a state of semiliteracy and ignorance by the region's school systems. Reconstruction governments in the South had instituted public schools for black and white alike. In the Jim Crow era, separate black and white school systems were organized. All education in the South was underfunded in comparison to the rest of the country (and is to this day), but the state funding of black schools was only a small fraction of the amount allotted to whites. In addition, in rural areas black children were only allowed to attend school for about half of the normal school year, so that they would be available in the fields for spring planting and the fall harvest. In Mississippi in the 1920s, Gov. Theodore Bilbo was heard to say that educating a black child "would only ruin a good field hand." Those words should come back to us today, when experts ponder the "mystery" of African-American students' lower scores on standardized tests.

The Thirteenth Amendment to the U.S. Constitution had made the former slaves and their descendants into U.S. citizens. But under Jim Crow, black citizenship was rendered meaningless. Black people could not vote, and so they could not serve on juries. This ensured that no black person could ever win in a legal dispute involving a white man and that white men would often go unpunished for criminal offenses against blacks. Lynchings and beatings of blacks by whites were rarely prosecuted, and when they were, the white defendants usually went free. So it was that the courts became another arm of the system enforcing white power and black powerlessness. And to this day, African-Americans, on average, are more suspicious of the criminal justice system than whites and more likely to receive unfair treatment from it.

The only positive difference between slavery and Jim Crow was that in a state of nominal freedom, blacks were able to conduct their family lives, community associations, and churches without white interference. Those were the zones of freedom. In those zones, black families and communities nurtured a culture of mutual aid and self-respect rooted in Christian faith. In addition, under Jim Crow, a few businesses arose to serve needs of the black community that white merchants would not serve (funeral homes, barber shops, etc.). A few black preachers (though only a few) were able to live off the donations of their church members. This small group of self-sufficient black professionals and businesspeople provided a core of independent leaders who were not directly accountable to white power for their livelihoods.

We Shall Overcome

America's Third Great Awakening again made the condition of African-Americans the central moral and political issue of the day. This spiritual and democratic revival emerged from the African-American churches of the Deep South, beginning in 1955 with the Montgomery, Alabama, bus boycott. This Great Awakening, which we know as the civil rights movement, was, among its black Southern leaders and foot soldiers, distinguished by a powerful and deeply-rooted faith in the whole truth of the Bible. Most African-American Christians have always believed that Jesus died and was risen to save us from our sins, but they have also always believed, with equal fervor, that the God who had become flesh in Jesus Christ was still the God of the Exodus—come to bring liberation to the enslaved. The God of the black churches was still the God of the prophets for whom righteousness was displayed as social justice. In the black churches, the kingdom of God, in which the normal order of wealth and power is reversed, had always been a promise for the future but also a goal for the present.

This holistic and truly orthodox Christianity had been the African-American gospel for hundreds of years. It exploded as a potent social force when a young minister named Dr. Martin Luther King, Jr. combined it with a profoundly Christian method of collective action for political power. The new tool was nonviolent resistance, a method King had discovered in his graduate school study of Mohandas Gandhi.

While its practitioners are not always Christian by name, the Gandhian philosophy of nonviolent resistance is, in Christian terms, a practical attempt to harness the spiritual power of Christ's crucifixion. It is rooted in the Christian insight that suffering, freely offered on behalf of others, is the way God works in the world. By standing for a righteous cause but refusing to vindicate its righteousness through violence, the nonviolent resister follows the way of Jesus of Nazareth who, through suffering and humiliation, was revealed as the Son of God.

King learned all this in his doctoral program at Boston University. He first preached it during the Montgomery bus boycott, at Dexter Avenue Baptist Church, in the midst of a Christian community struggling for its basic human rights. When that happened, Gandhianism found its natural home in African-American Christianity.

For the next ten years, African-Americans, joined by an ever-growing number of white allies, walked the streets and highways of the Deep South to claim their rights as children of God and citizens of the United States. They confronted American white supremacy at its most concentrated spot, where it had the power of state and local governments and police behind it. They confronted this armed power without any physical weapons. They were beaten and imprisoned, even killed, and accepted suffering as the price of justice. In the process, they caused a revolution in U.S. racial attitudes and practices.

In December 1955, when Rosa Parks kept her seat on that Montgomery bus, the average white American (outside the South) was deeply complacent and even apathetic about the condition of African-Americans. True, the previous year the Supreme Court had ruled that school desegregation was unconstitutional, and that had struck a panic into Southern whites. But the Court had also left the desegregation remedy to be carried out "with all deliberate speed," an oxymoronic phrase that signaled to the rest of the country that no revolution was imminent. Stereotypically docile and ignorant Negroes—such as Amos and Andy and Jack Benny's servant, Rochester—were still the image of black America on TV, and nothing seemed likely to change.

Then came Montgomery, and the children who desegregated the Little Rock schools, and the lunch counter sit-ins, and the Freedom Rides that were ended with mob violence and mass detentions. Then things began to change. It was only when black people took action to claim their rights and confronted violent hatred and repression with nonviolent resistance that the country and the world took notice.

The black freedom movement, centered in the African-American churches, also sparked a revival of public action for justice among many white Christians. Church institutions, including the National Council of Churches (NCC) and the National Catholic Conference for Interracial Justice, offered prominent support to the civil rights movement. Both organizations were among the sponsors of the historic 1963 March on Washington. At that event, NCC President Rev. Eugene Carson Blake spoke for many white American Christians when he said, "Late, late we come ... to march behind and with those able leaders of the Negro Americans who, to the shame of almost every white American have alone and without us mirrored the suffering of the cross." William McGuire King, in a *Christian Century* book review, recalls that the NCC was a major financial supporter of the 1964 Freedom Summer.

In 1965, when Dr. Martin Luther King, Jr. called for clergy to come to Selma, Alabama, and march in support of the voting rights movement, priests, ministers, nuns, rabbis, and lay church activists flooded the little town from every corner of America. An Episcopal seminarian—Jonathan Daniels, a Unitarian minister—James Reeb, and a Catholic laywoman—Viola Liuzzo gave their lives in Alabama, victims of attacks by local white racists. The Rev. Theodore Hesburgh, a Catholic priest and president of the University of Notre Dame, served on the Civil Rights Commission that later investigated racial violence in the Deep South. For a few years, it actually seemed possible that, as journalist Milton Viorst wrote, "The power of love, as expressed through Christian nonviolence, could transform men's hearts."

By the early 1960s, there was an amazing new consensus in America. Apathy about the oppression of African-Americans became moral outrage. Suddenly, Jim Crow, which had been perfectly acceptable for seventy years, would have to go, and black Americans would have to be seated at the main table of the American feast. The change was swift and visible in government, politics, and culture. In the blink of an eye, Amos and Andy were replaced by Sidney Poitier and Bill Cosby; Martin Luther King, Jr. was dining at the White House and winning the Nobel Peace Prize; and a Southern president (Lyndon Johnson) was telling the nation, "We shall overcome." Black mayors were elected in U.S. cities for the first time. A black man was appointed to the Supreme Court—Thurgood Marshall, who as an attorney had argued the landmark school desegregation case, *Brown v. the Board of Education*.

Then in the blink of another eye, it was 1968; King was dead, and momentum for social change, which had seemed so unstoppable two years earlier, was dying, too.

Awakening from the Dream

How did these startling changes in U.S. racial attitudes come about? Why did they happen in the first half of the 1960s? And why did the era of hope and change end so suddenly?

These are interesting historical questions, but they are much more than that. Four decades later, the racial status quo in America is still essentially that of 1969—formal equality and an atmosphere of tolerance overlaying deep inequalities in the actual conditions of life for most blacks and whites.

To the first two questions, we can say that the changes made by the civil rights movement were in large part the result of a genuine change of heart among many white Americans, brought out about by the moral power of nonviolent resistance. But a change of heart rarely takes place in a vacuum. The 1950s and early 1960s in America were marked by two overarching realities—the Cold War and an unprecedented period of economic growth and prosperity. Both provided an impetus for reform in America's racial practices and helped prepare the way for the country's political and corporate establishment to welcome the end of legal segregation.

On the Cold War front, the treatment of black people in the South was a major propaganda problem for the United States. In our competition with the Communist-ruled Soviet Union around the world, we claimed to be deserving of trust and support not simply because we were stronger and richer, but because democracy and capitalism were demonstrably better than one-party rule and economic centralization. This argument was especially crucial in the new nations of Africa and Asia that were choosing their post-colonial path. The impoverishment, exploitation, and disenfranchisement of millions of African-Americans made the virtues of democracy much harder to sell to people of color around the world, especially after the civil rights movement forced racist violence out of the shadows and onto the world's television screens. In the early 1960s, the end of segregation in the South and some accommodation of African-American political aspirations served the overriding interest of U.S. foreign policy.

On the economic front, in the 1950s cotton production in the

South was mechanized. The large, and mostly black, rural South-ern labor force was no longer needed and had begun dispersing to the big cities of the North. Also, with the arrival of interstate highways and air-conditioning, the South was becoming more integrated into the national economy. But Southern racial cus-toms Joint Center for Economic and the low level of public edu-cation that came with them were a major obstacle to the South's economic modernization. For these reasons, American big busi-ness also welcomed the death of Jim Crow.

The end of legal segregation and the reenfranchisement of black voters brought the South into conformity with the rest of the U.S. and removed the visible blight from America's image overseas. To the wielders of political and economic power, that was quite enough racial reform for one century.

In the decades since 1968, the stalling of progress toward sub-stantial equality for black people has sometimes been blamed on the assassination of Martin Luther King, Jr. The loss of the leader who had framed the strategy of the movement and articulated its goals was certainly a setback. King was a figure of historic propor-tions, deserving his place in the American pantheon alongside Washington and Lincoln. The 1970s and '80s would have been different with him on the scene. But the achievements of the early 1960s were possible because of the confluence of King's leader-ship, the heroic sacrifices of his black Southern constituents, and the powerful political and economic interests served by limited racial reform. The last two years of King's life demonstrate that once that last element was removed, the dragons of injustice became much more difficult to slay.

In the late 1960s—after legal segregation was abolished, black voting rights were secured, and racial discrimination in housing and employment were banned—Martin Luther King, Jr. began leading the civil rights movement in new directions. He began organizing a multiracial movement of poor people to demand new structures of economic equality in America—full employment and a guaranteed annual income for a start. At the same time, King took a leadership role in opposition to America's brutal anticommunist war in Vietnam. In other words, he set himself on collision courses with the business interests and Cold Warriors who had welcomed his leadership against Southern segregation.

Some analysts and many of King's movement colleagues have suggested that King's increasingly anticapitalist and antimilitarist direction may have provided the motive for his assassination. That is ultimately unknowable, but we do know that in the last two years of his life, King was no longer a welcome figure in the halls of power. If he had lived, this would not have changed. His presence would have brought moral authority and strategic wisdom to the subsequent movement for justice and peace. And no one since him has been nearly so effective a spokesperson for those causes. But we can't say with any certainty that the outcomes of the past four decades would have been terribly different.

One thing Martin Luther King, Jr. could not have changed was the end of America's post-World War II economic expansion. And that changed everything else. In 1973, wage growth for the average U.S. worker, which had been rapid and continuous for the previous twenty-five years, abruptly stopped. More than thirty years later, growth in real wages for hourly workers (adjusted for inflation) still has not resumed.

In the 1960s, much of the optimism about building a more just and equal society was founded on the assumption that economic growth would continue to make it possible to improve the condition of those at the bottom of society without requiring any real sacrifices from those at the top. This was a short-lived illusion, and when it faded, so did much of the political will for additional social and economic reform.

The period leading up to the 1960s had seen the formation of a large white middle class based mostly upon high-paying manufacturing jobs. The members of this blue-collar middle class were able to send their children to college to become white-collar managers and professionals. But the stagnation of wages and the disappearance of most manufacturing jobs from U.S. shores that began in the 1970s removed the bottom rungs from America's economic ladder at precisely the moment that most black Americans were poised to gain their first foothold.

In brief, when legal segregation was ended and economic stagnation set in, African-Americans were supposed by most whites to be free and empowered, but they were, in fact, still mostly very poor, undereducated and ill-prepared for life in the twenty first century. In the brief period of reform in the 1960s, very little was actually done to redress the injustices from three hundred years of slavery and another one hundred years of forced ignorance and poverty. When that era passed, most white Americans assumed that the country's playing field was now level. And it was. But, to use a football analogy, some of the players (most of the white ones) had the latest and best training and equipment, while others (most of the black ones) were still playing with turn-of-the-century leather helmets and no shoulder pads.

Chapter 6

The Racial Landscape of the Twenty-first Century

More than a half-century after the civil rights revolution, America's racial landscape is one of paradoxes. More than ever, black people are entering the mainstream of American life, and even the upper-middle-class of managers and professionals. More than ever the daily lives of many African-Americans and whites have much in common. Many of us live in the same kinds of subdivision houses. We drive the same SUVs, shop at the same big-box retail outlets, and eat at the same fast-food places. We vacation at the same amusement parks, and white and black teenagers irritate their parents with the same rap music.

At the same time, a large number of African-Americans are trapped in ever-deeper poverty and falling further behind the American mainstream. Even middle-class black people continue to experience daily discrimination and encounter subtle barriers to equality that white Americans never see. Perhaps as a result, the gap between black and white perceptions of America's racial reality is persistent and even growing.

Persistence of poverty among many African-Americans is the most troubling feature of the new century's racial landscape. And poverty is persisting despite historic progress for many other African-Americans. One study (reported in the *Minneapolis-St. Paul Star Tribune*) found that, from the early 1970s to the mid-1990s, the number of affluent black households earning more than $75,000 increased almost six times over. "But that's only half the story," the report continued. "Among blacks as a whole, these gains were offset by entrenched poverty at the lower end of the economic scale."

Henry Louis Gates, Jr., Chair of the Afro-American Studies Department at Harvard, put it this way in an interview for the PBS program, *Frontline*: "The central paradox confronting our generation of African-Americans is this: We have simultaneously . . . the largest black middle class in history and the largest black underclass in history. Forty-five percent of all black children live at or beneath the poverty line." "Nobody predicted this in 1968," Gates continued. "We thought that if we could move into the middle class to [this] extent . . . , then everybody would be in the middle class. Thurgood Marshall told his associates the day of Brown v. Board [of Education], 'It's all over now, boys. [In] five years we won't even need the NAACP, we won't even need advocacy groups, we will all be members of the American mainstream.' And as we know all too painfully that didn't take place."

The African-American poor are now heavily concentrated in inner-city neighborhoods where almost everyone is poor. Those districts have little power when, for instance, school funding is handed out. And, among the middle class mainstream, the political will to deliver quality health care to people who can't pay for it is always weak. This forms a vicious cycle since bad education and health care make it ever more unlikely that the children of the next generation will rise out of poverty.

Due to its status as media capital, the case of unequal services in New York City is especially well documented. In a recent series on disparities of social class in America, *The New York Times* found that the infant death rate in predominantly African-American East Harlem is forty-two per thousand, which is high even by the standards of poor countries. As former Senator Bill Bradley noted, "A child's chances of surviving to age five are better in Bangladesh than in East Harlem."

The nonprofit United Hospital Fund of New York City has reported that, in the heavily black and Hispanic South Bronx, 531 infants out of every 1,000 born require neonatal hospitalization, compared to 69 out of 1,000 in a middle-class suburb. To child development experts, that high rate of neonatal crisis suggests high rates of retardation and brain damage among those same children as they grow.

The New York Times reports described some public hospitals in which there were no working microscopes to study tissue samples and no gauze or syringes to collect blood samples. A physician at the city's Bellevue Hospital reported that a few years ago, "We were running out of sutures in the operating room." About the same time, Harlem Hospital ran out of penicillin.

Five years down the line, all those babies who were born sick, in ill-equipped hospitals, will hit inner-city school systems. There they will get little help in overcoming the deficits of poverty. In his book, *Savage Inequalities*, educator and author Jonathan Kozol found a near-perfect correspondence between the race and class of a New York community's residents and the annual per-pupil expenditure of its public schools. $5,590 per year is spent on a child in the Bronx and Harlem, $6,340 for the nonwhite kids of Roosevelt, $6,400 for the working-class black kids of Mount Vernon, $7,400 for the slightly better-off community of Yonkers, and over $11,000 for the almost exclusively white children of Manhasset, Jericho, and Great Neck—affluent communities on Long Island.

And this is not just a New York phenomenon. The U.S. Department of Education found that nationwide, the wealthiest school districts spent 56 percent more per child than the poorest ones. Nationwide, we also find that black children are three times as likely as white children to be placed in classes for the mentally retarded, but only half as likely to be placed in classes for the gifted.

The High Cost of Living Black

Many of the problems described so far are functions of poverty, not simply of race. The same patterns of poor health care and low education spending seen in predominantly African-American communities can be found to some degree in low income communities of any ethnic group. But there are other barriers to equality that seem to be purely matters of old-fashioned, institutionalized racism.

For instance, a report by a consumer group, the Center for Responsible Lending, studied "payday lenders," who entrap consumers desperate for cash into triple-digit-interest loans. The group found that such lenders tend to locate their stores in predominantly African-American neighborhoods. At first, that may not seem surprising. After all, blacks are disproportionately poor, and poor people are more likely to need cash. But the Center, which studied black neighborhoods in North Carolina, found that "even after controlling for variables associated with the industry's purported customer base, such as income and home-ownership . . . African-American neighborhoods have three times as many payday lenders per capita as white neighborhoods."

In recent years, civil rights lawyers and consumer groups have discovered that African-American car buyers are charged more to finance their purchase than are whites with the same income and credit score. Investigators have learned that the auto finance industry uses a two-part formula when computing the interest rate offered on auto loans. The first part is known as the "buy rate." This rate is determined by a computerized credit rating system controlled by the lender and based strictly on credit and risk factors. The computerized system gives a minimum interest rate, called the "buy rate," to the dealer which constitutes the lender's authorization to give the customer the loan at that rate.

The second part of the loan rate is known as the "markup," which can boost the final interest rate on the auto loan offered to the customer. The markup goes not to the lender, but to the dealer, and it has nothing to do with the customer's creditworthiness or the cost of processing the loan. It simply represents the dealer's estimation of what he can get out of the customer. It is the markup that is widely used to hike the loan cost for African-American car buyers.

In California, civil rights groups and consumers, led by Clinton administration civil rights chief Bill Lann Lee, filed a suit challenging the practice by auto dealers. The California groups found that the average markup paid by black car buyers was close to $1,000, while the average amount paid by whites was less than $500.

For years racial profiling by police, especially for traffic stops, has been a widespread complaint among African-American men. They joke bitterly about being pulled over for "DWB"—driving while black. The American Civil Liberties Union, which fought a number of cases challenging the use of race as a criteria for supposedly random checks by police, has compiled data studies from around the country showing large differences in the rate of stops and searches for African-Americans and other nonwhite groups.

As recently as 2006, according to the *Daily Tribune* in Columbia, Missouri, statistics on traffic stops in Missouri still showed that black drivers are pulled over at a higher rate than whites. According to a 2001 Gallup poll, most Americans agree that racial profiling by police exists. But Gallup found that only 55 percent of whites believe racial profiling is widespread, while 83 percent of blacks said it is.

Such wide gaps in perception between black and white Americans are a persistent feature of public opinion polling. For instance, in 2005, the aftermath of Hurricane Katrina revealed a deep racial divide in perceptions of social reality. In a Pew Center survey, two-thirds of African-Americans said that the government would have responded more quickly and effectively if more of the Katrina victims had been white. Fewer than one in five whites agreed with that statement.

These wide and persistent gaps in perception may prove nothing one way or another about the social equality of blacks and whites, but they do prove that, beneath the surface of America's real racial progress, we are still two nations, with a long way to go before we meet at what Martin Luther King called "the table of brotherhood."

For a more concrete measure of the real differences between the lives of black and whites in America today, we need look no further than *The State of Black America*, a report compiled every year by the Urban League, a civil rights group focused on economic empowerment. The report compares the status of African-Americans and whites in areas such as income, education, health care, wealth, and business ownership. The Urban League staff uses this information to compute an overall Equality Index. In 2006, for instance, the Equality Index was .73, with the average white American figured as 1.0. This meant that, in the Urban League's estimate, the average white American received 27 percent more of the nation's goods and benefits than the average black American.

Over recent years, *The State of Black America* has shown slow but steady gains in household income among African-Americans. But the significance of those gains is belied by the most depressing figure in the report—the relative wealth of black and white households. According to the Urban League, in 2006, the median net worth of the average African-American family was ten times less than that of the average white family. The numbers were $6,166 net worth for black households versus $67,000 for whites.

The Urban League attributed this difference partly to gaps in income—the poorest people, who, as we have seen, are disproportionately black, are more likely to be living in debt, and so would show a negative net worth. The wealth gap also reflects the fact that upper-middle-class blacks are more often the first generation of their families to attain affluence. Unlike their professional peers, they don't benefit from parental gifts, loans, or inheritances to, for instance, buy their first home. The difference in home ownership rates (50 percent for blacks and 70 percent for whites) was identified by the Urban League as the second main source of the wealth gap.

The wealth statistic is important. Even if income, education, life-expectancy, and all the other gaps were closed overnight, the wealth gap would remain because wealth is accrued and passed down over generations. And wealth is power. Income is not necessarily power. As we all know, most income disappears almost immediately into consumption. Wealth stays and grows. It can make things happen. Wealth—whether a portfolio of stocks and bonds, or equity in a home—can serve as collateral for a business loan. It can endow a charitable foundation or an educational institution. Or it can simply allow parents and grandparents to leave an inheritance which will give their descendants a head start in life.

The enormity of the wealth gap between black and white families should be enough, in and of itself, to convince us that real equality is still decades or even generations away.

Chapter 7

Where to Start? Sources for a Faithful Response to Racism

The Bible in Black and White

In the years immediately after World War II, Clarence Jordan was a promising young Southern Baptist minister, recently married, with a brand new doctorate in New Testament Greek. But instead of taking on a pastorate, Jordan, whose undergraduate degree was in agriculture, returned to his native land of southwest Georgia and, with another white family, established a cooperative farm that they called "Koinonia," the Greek word for "fellowship." Jordan and his friends hoped that Koinonia, located in Sumter County near the town of Americus, would become an island of racial reconciliation in the sea of Southern Jim Crow and offer economic development alternatives for the area's desperately poor population.

Koinonia was founded on three principles that Jordan saw as the core of New Testament Christianity: the brotherhood of all people, a rejection of violence in any form (including military service), and the sharing of income and possessions. Anyone of any color who embraced those principles was welcome to join Koinonia Community.

From the very beginning, the white Koinonians deliberately set about defying the codes of Southern segregation. Black and white sat together at the dinner table. Interracial groups gathered for Bible study. At the same time, Jordan began farming the land and offering his agricultural expertise to his poor neighbors. The Koinonia residents became members of a local Baptist congregation. Jordan's wife Florence taught Sunday School. He led the singing and occasionally preached. There were problems on the farm and in the fledgling community, but in its essentials, the Koinonia vision was taking flesh. The believers held all in common, as they had in Jerusalem; and as at Nazareth, the good news was proclaimed to the poor.

So persecution was, perhaps, inevitable. It began in 1950 when the Koinonia residents were excommunicated from their church for their racial attitudes and practices. After the Supreme Court decision on school desegregation in 1954, southern segregationists circled the wagons and even mild dissent was no longer tolerated. The Ku Klux Klan and the White Citizens' Council took a more aggressive strategy against Koinonia. The Farm and its residents came under a complete economic boycott. Koinonia children were harassed at the local schools. Then, in 1956, Jordan helped two black students who were seeking to enroll in all-white Georgia State College, and the campaign against Koinonia turned violent. The Farm was repeatedly fired on from passing vehicles. Koinonia's roadside produce stand was bombed. A local merchant who violated the boycott against Koinonia had his store bombed. Intruders came onto Koinonia's property and cut down three hundred pecan trees. Vehicles were ruined by sugar placed in gasoline tanks.

Despite all of this hardship, the residents of Koinonia never retreated from their Christian witness to racial equality. In 1955, when the boycott and intimidation campaign was well under way, the Farm began an interracial summer camp. In 1962, when the community at Koinonia was down to four adult members and the farm was scarcely functioning, Jordan went to march for racial equality and was arrested with his fellow Baptist preacher, Dr. Martin Luther King, Jr., in nearby Albany, Georgia.

In the late 1950s and early 1960s, the violence against Koinonia drew national publicity, and as a result, Clarence Jordan was invited to speak at many church-related conferences and events around the country. He always spoke from Scripture. With a Greek New Testament in his hand, he would deliver off-the-cuff translations into colloquial English, interspersed with real-time commentary. This approach had the effect of bringing the clash of values recounted in the gospels, Acts, and the epistles into clear focus around contemporary issues of racism, war, wealth, and poverty. People began asking him to write down his biblical renderings.

Finally, in 1963, with the South exploding in racial crisis and Koinonia's farming operations crippled by boycotts and violence, Clarence Jordan retreated to an unused farm outbuilding in the middle of a field and began writing what he called a "Cotton Patch" version of the New Testament.

In these books, Jordan not only translated the words of Scripture into conversational English, but he also translated the time from the first century to the twentieth and the places from the Mediterranean basin to the southern United States. The state of Georgia became the territory of Palestine, and so the world learned about Jesus of Valdosta, who was born in Gainesville and executed in Atlanta.

Later, in the book of Acts, Jordan's readers saw Saul struck with a vision of Christ when he had "stopped for gas just outside of Chattanooga." Later he and Barney (Barnabas) began their missionary journeys by taking a bus from Atlanta to Pensacola. Eventually Paul spread the gospel all the way to Rome, which, of course, was Washington, D.C.

There was much more going on in Jordan's translations than mere regional novelty. He also translated theological concepts into readily accessible twentieth century terms. The Greek word *logos*, rendered as "the Word" in traditional translations, is "the Idea" in Jordan's version. And, in his gospel of John, when the Idea becomes flesh and dwells among us, it parks its trailer next to ours (from the Greek word that means "pitched his tent"). Jesus the Messiah is called the Leader, and the kingdom of God is called "the God Movement."

Jordan's real stroke of exegetical genius came with his rendering of "Jew" and "Gentile." In the Cotton Patch, the Jews are white people. Devoutly religious Jews are White American Protestants (abbreviated WAP). Gentiles, Samaritans, and other despised outsiders are blacks. With that simple transposition, a curtain was lifted from the biblical text. The ordinary reader was able to see, probably for the first time, that the issue of ethnicity and culture (the stuff we call "race") was a central theme of the entire New Testament.

The theme emerges almost from the start, in Luke 3:7-9, when John the Baptizer preaches, "Don't start patting one another on the back with that 'we-good-white-people' stuff, because I'm telling you that if God wants to, he can make white folks out of this pile of rocks." At the start of Jordan's Luke 15, Jesus of Valdosta was consorting with "'nigger-lovers' and black people" and "the white church people and Sunday school teachers were raising Cain."

But the theme of race really takes over the narrative in Jordan's book of Acts, which he calls "The Happenings." Here the spread of the God Movement among the Gentiles becomes the fever of liberation among Southern blacks. The controversy with the Judaizers—who wanted Gentile Christians to abide by Jewish custom and law—becomes a battle over segregation and the traditions associated with white supremacy. In the Cotton Patch Happenings, with the apostles placed on Southern city streets and using motorized transport, it is easy to forget whether one is reading a chronicle of the first churches or a diary, circa 1961, of the founding days of the Student Nonviolent Coordinating Committee (SNCC).

In Acts 10, Peter, whose name Jordan translates literally as

"Rock," has his vision of "unclean" foods. The next day he is taken to visit a black army officer named Captain Cornwall. When Cornwall calls Rock "mister," Rock replies, "Don't 'mister' me, for I am a human being the same as you." Rock continues, "Y'all understand how uncustomary it is for a white man to socialize or stay with people of a different race, don't you? . . . but as for me, God has made it plain as day that I'm never to think of any man as inferior or no good. . . . I am convinced beyond any doubt that God pays no attention to a man's skin" (Luke-Acts).

After Paul and Barney have been all over the South, from north Florida to Louisiana, gathering mixed groups of black and white believers, the racial controversy comes to a head. They are called back to Atlanta (Acts 15) where "some church members who believed in segregation got up and said, 'They [the black believers] have got to be told to accept segregation and all the traditional rules.'" But "after a heated discussion," Rock settles the issue. "They [the blacks], exactly the same as we, are saved by the undeserved favor of the Lord Jesus."

James, the brother of Jesus, whom Jordan calls, "Jim," elaborates, "We should not pester people from other races who are turning to God, but should advise them to . . . be extremely sensitive to and considerate of immature whites who have not outgrown their traditions, since for generations these customs have been advocated on every Sabbath in every church throughout the South."

For most people, in most places and times, the social dynamite Clarence Jordan found in the book of Acts has been hidden behind arcane, undecipherable talk about circumcision and food sacrificed to idols. By placing the particulars of the story in his own time and place, Jordan jarred Christians into recognizing the universal, theological truth behind those ancient Jewish peculiarities. That truth was, simply put, this: The first business of the God Movement in history is to obliterate the false distinctions people draw among themselves. There are to be no more in-groups and out-groups. There are no more chosen people. There will be no master races or subject peoples. The aim of the God Movement is to draw all humanity together into one family under a common Parent.

Two thousand years later, it may be impossible for us to imagine what a revolution this was in human history. Catholic anthropologist Rene Girard has suggested that the entire foundation of human civilization lies in the creation of national identities by an "in" group scapegoating an "out" group. It was a process that began among competing clans of hunter-gatherers and, perhaps, reached its absurd apex in the twentieth century with the Holocaust and the Cold War threat of nuclear obliteration.

Ancient religions mostly served to reinforce the scapegoating process. Gods were tribal gods, limited by territory and culture. Priesthoods beseeched the god of one people to conquer the god of another. Throughout much of the Hebrew Bible, the God of the Jews is seen in this light, though in the later books of the prophets, Judaism had conceived the notion that its God was universal.

According to Girard's thesis, the advent of Christianity has been the only thing to slow or interrupt this process of creating enemy nations and inferior races. Christianity, at least in its doctrines, does not create scapegoats; instead it places the scapegoat—the innocent crucified Lord—on the throne of the universe. It does not exalt one group by pitting it against another; instead it seeks to gather all people into unity through an ethic of self-sacrifice.

For two thousand years now, this Christian universalism has been loose in the world. In recent centuries, it has appeared in a variety of secular translations. But it is still the essential Christian Idea. As we begin looking for ways to act faithfully in a society infected by racism, we can begin, as Clarence Jordan did, with the understanding that eliminating racial sin is absolutely central to all Christian faith and practice. It should be, for us, what it has been for believers from Jerusalem to Georgia—a question not just of politics or social action, but of orthodoxy.

In our world, unlike that of Bible times, considerations of race are also bound up with a history of slavery and institutionalized injustice. This, of course, means that the entire weight of biblical teaching on justice for the poor and oppressed—from the law of Moses through the prophets and on down to Jesus' Nazareth proclamation of the Jubilee (Luke 4)—pushes Christians to become advocates for equality and for the righting of America's racial wrongs.

African-American Biblical Theology

From the earliest days of slavery, African-Americans have presented their case for liberation and equality in biblical and Christian terms. The biblical and theological understanding of American history and society that comes down to us through the African-American tradition is essential to any American Christian understanding of racism. African-American Christians, who have often been nearly as powerless as Christ on the cross, have given us a way to see our country through the eyes of Christ.

The African-American spirituals and the traditions of African-American preaching present a theology rooted in a confidence that God is on the side of the poor and powerless. The slaves heard the biblical story, clearly, as one of slaves liberated and suffering redeemed. For the slave, the central passage of Scripture is contained in one of the most important spiritual songs, "Let my people go." Moses speaks, reporting directly from the mouth of God, and tells one of the most powerful men on earth that God's people are not meant to be enslaved. And God acts in mighty ways to free His people and restore them to their proper place and status.

In the 1970s, James Cone and other African-American theologians deemed the Exodus event to be the central truth in what they called "Black Theology." At the same time, Peruvian priest Gustavo Guttieriez, author of *A Theology of Liberation*, was proclaiming the Exodus to be the signal event in the theology of colonized and oppressed Latin America. Both of these Christian thinkers were expressing the perception, rooted in Scripture, that God is always active in the events of history—everyday history, religious history, and political history alike. When they look at the story of Israel in the Hebrew Bible, they see God bringing his people out of slavery, forming them into a nation, and persistently correcting their lapses into injustice and idolatry through the ministry of the prophets.

In the New Testament, God so completely identifies with the suffering of the poor and oppressed that in Jesus, God becomes one of them. God proclaims the primacy of the poor and oppressed in the plan of history (see Luke 4 and Matthew 5, for instance). And God remains on earth, permanently resident among the homeless, hungry, and imprisoned (Matthew 25). God suffers a painful death, unjustly, at the hands of political and religious power and so redeems the suffering of every victim of oppression.

In African-American theology, as in the liberation theology of mostly-Catholic Latin America, the Resurrection is seen as a fulfillment of the Exodus. God, who triumphed over the particular power of the Egyptians in a certain time and place, triumphs permanently over every oppressive, life-denying force in the universe. As African-American Catholic church historian Cyprian Davis puts it, "Black theology reaches its zenith with the paschal mystery. The mystery of Christ's suffering and death has been lived by us as a people, but by sharing in this mystery we share also in his glorification."

This means that working for the freedom and dignity of each person is at the very heart of what it means to be Christian. That vocation is acted out in our particular places and times. In the United States, it has been most particularly acted out in the redemptive suffering and struggle of God's enslaved, oppressed, and despised African-American people. This is what Dr. Martin Luther King, Jr. meant when he declared that the job of his organization, the Southern Christian Leadership Council (SCLC), was "to save the soul of America." He was not coining a polemical metaphor. He was speaking, straightforwardly, in biblical Christian theology. As James Cone has put it, white racism is America's original sin. And the struggle against it is, for all of us, one of the main arenas of our redemption.

The Teaching of the Churches

In the years since 1968, the leaders of America's predominantly white Christian churches have put the question of racism before their people as a matter of faith. Through pastoral letters, convention resolutions, and policy statements, the churches, in their teaching function, have sought to help American Christians, especially white ones, to see racism as a social, economic, and spiritual reality in their daily lives and the life of the nation. Over and over our churches have declared that racism is a sin, an affront to the doctrine that each person is made in the image of God.

In their 1979 pastoral letter, *Brothers and Sisters to Us,* the U.S. Catholic Bishops declared:

Racism is a sin; a sin that divides the human family, blots out the image of God among specific members of that family, and violates the fundamental human dignity of those called to be children of the same Father. Racism is the sin that says some human beings are inherently superior and others essentially inferior because of races. It is the sin that makes racial characteristics the determining factor for the exercise of human rights. It mocks the words of Jesus: "Treat others the way you would have them treat you." Indeed, racism is more than a disregard for the words of Jesus; it is a denial of the truth of the dignity of each human being revealed by the mystery of the Incarnation.

Contemporary church teaching defines racism as not just wrong attitudes and actions by individuals, but as a system of oppression. The formulation used by the Episcopal bishops of the U.S. in their 1994 pastoral letter *The Sin of Racism* is typical. It holds that "the essence of racism is prejudice coupled with power." Christian leaders also acknowledge the reality of structural or institutional racism that is far more powerful than any hateful individual. In its 1999 document, *Facing Racism: A Vision of the Beloved Community*, the Presbyterian Church (U.S.A.) declared:

> Racism is nurtured and sustained by systemic power. Power must be understood in social, not individual terms.... Historically, institutions have tended to be preferential to some group or groups in comparison to others. . . . Rewards are based on group membership not personal attitude. Consequently, all Whites benefit from racism "whether or not they have ever committed a racist act, uttered a racist word, or had a racist thought."

Because of this unavoidable complicity, confession and repentance are also common themes in teachings on race from the predominantly white churches. As reported in a World Council of Churches document, in its *Charter for Racial Justice Policies*, the United Methodist Church states, "We are conscious that 'we have sinned as our ancestors did; we have been wicked and evil' (Psalm 106:6). We are called to a renewed commitment to the elimination of institutional racism." The Episcopal bishops "acknowledge our participation in this sin [of racism] and . . . lament its corrosive effects on our lives. We repent of this sin, and ask God's grace and forgiveness."

Just as in our individual relationships with God and each other, confession and repentance must be followed by concrete action to right the wrongs of the past and build a more just future. Almost all of the U.S. Christian churches have put the weight of their lobbying offices and social action committees behind public policies to ameliorate the effects of racism. In its 1988 statement, *The Church and Racism*, Pope John Paul II's Pontifical Commission on Peace and Justice put a priority on building solidarity among people of all races—at the individual, church and social levels—and demanded, "The victims of racism, wherever they may be, must be defended."

Such penitence often leads churches to reorder their internal priorities. The Evangelical Lutheran Church in America (ELCA) was founded in 1988 by the uniting of several smaller Lutheran communions. Shortly after its founding, the ELCA adopted a goal that "within the first ten years of its existence, ten percent of this church's membership would be African American, Asian, Hispanic, or Native American." The Presbyterian Church (U.S.A.) document on *Facing Racism* came with a detailed set of actions to be taken at the national, regional, and local levels to put flesh on that denomination's commitment to become an "inclusive community."

In every Christian denomination and tradition, there is a clear, authoritative, and powerful body of theological and pastoral teaching and reflection which we can adapt to our local circumstances. As we have seen, the best teaching of the churches tells us that in the American context, a faithful response to racism will require that we begin by acknowledging the wrongs of the past, seeing how they continue into the present, and attempting to set them right. In doing this, we should look for strategies that build up the bonds of solidarity among people of different racial groups, both at the face-to-face community level and in the life of the nation.

Chapter 8

The First Step: Confession

Bridging divisions between people always begins with acknowledging the wrongs of the past. This is true at the personal level. When there is sin, there has to be confession, followed by penance. When sin is confessed and the sinner is willing to make amends, forgiveness and healing follow. When there is conflict in a family, a marriage, or a friendship, someone has to apologize before it is possible to move on.

The same thing is true among peoples and nations. That's why the German government today still makes an annual payment of reparations to the Jewish state of Israel. Closer to home, that's why it has been important, in the Deep South, to prosecute forty-year-old racist murders from the civil rights era. That is why, in 1985, Pope John Paul II traveled to West Africa and made a statement of penitence for African slavery on behalf of the Catholic Church. The pope's apology was repeated in Santo Domingo in 1992 and as part of the jubilee liturgy of repentance at the Vatican in 2000. That is also why, in 2005, the U.S. Senate passed a resolution apologizing, as a body, for its failure throughout the twentieth century to pass antilynching legislation that could have saved the lives of hundreds of African-American men.

Perhaps the strongest and clearest example of the power of confession to heal a nation comes from postapartheid South Africa. Apartheid was the system by which a 15 percent minority of white South Africans exerted complete and often brutal domination over the country's black majority. During the struggle to end apartheid, many white South Africans expressed a fear that if the system ever fell, there would be a bloodbath as black Africans took revenge. When the system finally did fall in 1991, there was no bloodbath, and there was no revenge. The transition to majority rule came peacefully, through an election. And that election was followed by an inspiring process of national reconciliation.

Rather than trying and imprisoning those who, under the old system, had committed human rights violations, the new government, elected by the black majority, instituted a Truth and Reconciliation Commission to investigate the crimes of the past. The Commission had subpoena power (the ability to force people to appear before it) and the power to grant pardons for past crimes. Anyone who came before the Truth and Reconciliation Commission and made a full and honest confession of his or her crimes received a pardon. Anyone who did not confess could be recommended for prosecution. One by one, and by the score, policemen, soldiers, and government intelligence agents came forth to confess that they had tortured prisoners, fired on unarmed civilians, and assassinated political opponents.

The result was an unprecedented, nonviolent cleansing of several decades of horrendous violence. To a large extent, South Africa was able to begin anew with a clean slate. Post-apartheid South Africa has a lot of very serious problems, but race-based resentment over the past is not one of them.

An American Truth Commission?

America's racial history cries out for our own "truth and reconciliation commission." After nearly four hundred years, we remain mired in division and resentment. We are, all of us, heirs to a system in which black families were intentionally destroyed, black children were denied education, and poor white workers were deliberately pitted against their black counterparts. To this day, many of our most intractable social and economic problems grow directly from that system. Yet most white Americans are ignorant of this history and resent any reference to it as an attempt to blame them for sins they never committed.

U.S. Rep. John Conyers of Michigan, the highest-ranking Democrat on the House Judiciary Committee, has proposed a truth commission for the U.S. In every session of Congress since 1989, Conyers has introduced a bill that would establish "a commission to study slavery and subsequent racial and economic discrimination against freed slaves [and] the impact of those forces on today's living African-Americans." According to Conyers, "The commission established would also shed light on the capture and procurement of slaves, the transport and sale of slaves, the treatment of slaves in the colonies and in the United States. It would examine the extent to which Federal and State governments in the U.S. supported the institution of slavery and examine federal and state laws that discriminated against freed African slaves from the end of the Civil War to the present." The commission Conyers proposes would also be directed to consider whether, and how, the federal government should apologize or make amends for any damages the commission may find.

Conyers acknowledges that there is strong opposition to an American truth commission. "Many people want to leave slavery in the past," he says. "They contend that slavery happened so long ago that it is hurtful and divisive to bring it up now." At a 2005 conference on "The Impact of Slavery on Today's African-Americans," Conyers noted, "Everyone profited from the labor of slaves, even later immigrants, because slave labor . . . built the infrastructure of this nation." In addition, he said, "The debt we talk about is not centuries old, but dates back only a few decades and is within our lifetimes because of Jim Crow."

The idea of a national commission to judge and set right the wrongs stemming from slavery may seem utopian and far-fetched, but it is worth remembering that Rep. Conyers is the same man who, in 1968, introduced a bill to make Martin Luther King's birthday a national holiday and continued to do so every year until it finally became law in 1983.

Why is the acknowledgment of past wrongs so important? As Mississippi novelist William Faulkner had one of his characters say in *Absalom, Absalom,* "The past is not dead. It's not even past." Faulkner was right. The past lives on among us through its consequences. And those consequences pass from generation to generation. Children who are abused are more likely to grow up to become abusers. Children whose parents are poorly educated are less likely to do well in school. These cycles can be broken, but breaking them requires deliberate action that begins with recognizing the problem. The past—whether of our family or our country—is a part of us. At least it is until we name it and deal with it.

Acts of Public Contrition

The process of naming past wrongs and beginning to set them right doesn't have to wait for national legislation. It can begin locally, and it already has. The city of Chicago has passed legislation requiring companies that do business with the city to research their history and declare any corporate association with slavery or the slave trade. This has led to public apologies to the descendants of enslaved African-Americans from J.P. Morgan Trust, Wachovia Bank, and Aetna Insurance for the ways in which those companies profited from slavery. The Community Race Relations Council of Waco, Texas, is leading a campaign to have the city and county governments adopt resolutions recognizing, in very specific terms, their complicity with lynchings of black men in the early twentieth century. In Jackson, Tennessee, in

2000, on the fortieth anniversary of the start of that city's civil rights movement, the local newspaper, *The Jackson Sun*, confessed that throughout the 1960s, it had failed to adequately and objectively cover the most important story in its community. To make amends, the newspaper had a team of reporters work to document the history of the Jackson civil rights movement. The results—which included a lengthy examination of the newspaper's own role during the civil rights years—were printed in a special edition of the newspaper and posted permanently on the paper's Web site.

Many church groups—from the Southern Baptist Convention to the Moravian Church and the Episcopal Church (U.S.A.)—have made public confessions of past complicity in slavery and racism as a beginning to new relationships between the races. The stories of some Catholic nuns illustrate how public acknowledgement of past wrongs can happen, and what it can accomplish.

The Sisters of Loretto were the first women's religious community founded in the United States. They began in central Kentucky in 1812 when that region was on the American frontier. In the next decades, they followed the frontier, establishing schools and convents in Arkansas, Missouri, Colorado, and points west.

"We're proud of our history," Sister of Loretto Joan Campbell told the *Louisville Courier Journal* in the summer of 2000. "We're the first U.S. community, and we're always carrying on about that."

While researching her order's proud history, however, Campbell stumbled upon some shame. In the nineteenth century, the Sisters of Loretto owned slaves—many slaves. In 1860, there were eighty enslaved people on the estate at the Kentucky motherhouse alone. They grew the food that fed the sisters and their students. They built the chapels, the schools, and the residences. They emptied the chamber pots and scrubbed the floors so that the sisters could lead lives devoted to prayer and service.

According to the historical record, the sisters did not buy or sell slaves. Usually families of the nuns and their students sent the slaves along with their daughters or offered them as contributions to the order. The sisters accepted these "gifts," and there is no record that they ever freed any of their slaves. The sisters baptized the slaves, gave them religious instruction, and taught many of them to read and write. Some of the female slaves even became auxiliary members of the order. The sisters were good and humane masters, exceptionally so by the standards of the time. But the fact remains that for five decades, their workers of African descent were never paid. They couldn't leave for another job. They had no rights. They were human property.

Today the Sisters of Loretto are known as staunch, impassioned advocates of social justice. Members of the order participated in the civil rights movement of the 1960s and the antiwar and human rights movements that followed. They pioneered in using the invested resources of the religious orders to promote corporate social responsibility. Some might say they've done more than their part to make up for the sins of the past. But confronted with the evidence Joan Campbell found, the sisters felt they should do more.

The first thing they did was collect as many of the names of the slaves as could be found in the order's archives. Then one of the sisters was commissioned to design and construct a monument to the slaves to be placed next to the sisters' cemetery at the motherhouse, where slaves were buried in unmarked graves.

In July 2000, two hundred sisters and associates gathered in Kentucky for the unveiling of the bronze monument, which includes a profile of an unnamed nineteenth-century African-American and all the known names of the slaves of the Sisters of Loretto. At the unveiling the name of each slave was read and the congregation responded, as in the litany of the saints, "Pray for us."

"We need to ask for their [the slaves'] forgiveness," Campbell said. "It's too late to now to do that in person, but we can ask for their intercession."

Later that same year, just before Christmas, the Sisters of Loretto were joined by members of two other religious orders—the Sisters of Charity of Nazareth and the Dominicans of St. Catharine—for a service of reconciliation with the descendants of slaves. All three orders were founded in the same region of Kentucky in the early 1800s, and all three shared a legacy of slaveholding. Four hundred people, black and white, gathered at St. Joseph's Church in Bardstown, Kentucky—a church built in 1819, in part by slaves. There the sisters made a formal apology to the African-American community of the region for the sins of the past and asked for forgiveness. And after a program of gospel singing and prayers of repentance, the forgiveness flowed.

"This is a glorious day," said Martha Hickman, a Bardstown African-American, to the sisters. "I cannot tell you what this service has done for me. It has strengthened my heart. My deceased ancestors are crying tears of joy in heaven today, and I'm sure yours are too." Elaine Riley, a black associate member of the Dominicans said simply, "We hear you. We share your sorrow, and we humbly accept your apology."

Chapter 9

Pushing the Buttons

A cknowledgment of the past through a process of confession and reconciliation is the starting place for racial justice in America. The next step is to take measures aimed at righting our racial wrongs.

How is it that the injustices of the past and their consequences continue into the present? And how may they be addressed? Here the warm feelings of reconciliation may break down, since analyzing problems and posing solutions inevitably leads to discussion of controversial, uncomfortable, and potentially divisive topics. But in order to begin resolving America's unfinished business, we must find ways to talk openly and constructively about these questions in a way that separates facts and reason from fear and resentment.

Two issues that cry out for an open airing and a fact-checking are the issues of black family patterns and the involvement of African-Americans in crime.

The Crisis Facing African-American Families

If you want proof of the disastrous consequences of not talking about an issue, you need look no further than the complex of questions surrounding the makeup and stability of African-American families.

In 1965, Daniel Moynihan, a Harvard sociologist who later became a Democratic senator from New York, attempted to sound an alarm over what he saw as a troubling rise in the rate of single-parent households and out-of-wedlock births among black Americans. In a report drafted for President Lyndon Johnson, Moynihan referred to the "pathology" of the black family. For this inflammatory language, Moynihan was accused of blaming the victims of injustice for their own sufferings. His report was discredited, and for two decades, few reputable scholars or commentators were willing to address the implications of the trend Moynihan had identified.

African-American author and sociologist William Julius Wilson was one of the first to break the post-Moynihan silence. He has pointed out that the income gap between the poorest and most affluent African-Americans is wider than the gap for Americans as a whole. Put simply, in the past three decades, many African-American households have done very well. But many others have fallen further and further behind.

One major factor in this growing income gap is education. For all races, the gap between people with a college degree and their high-school-educated counterparts has grown steadily for three decades. The other factor that Wilson found to distinguish persistently poor African-American families was the presence or absence of the father. Households headed by a single parent (usually a single mother) are far more likely to be poor than those headed by a married couple. In fact, in his study of poor neighborhoods in Chicago (*When Work Disappears*), Wilson found that families headed by a never-married mother had a median annual income that was less than one-fourth the amount for a married couple household. He also found that 31 percent of the persistently poor households in his study were headed by a black woman of childbearing age.

While since the 1970s the number of single-parent households has increased among all American groups, African-American households are still far more likely than white ones to be headed by a single parent. As of 2003, 62 percent of African-American children lived in single-parent households. For whites, the rate was 22 percent, and 34 percent for Hispanics. These statistics are not surprising when we also note that 70 percent of African-American babies are born out of wedlock. The national figure is 33 percent, and 25 percent for whites. And the phenomenon of single-parent families is self-perpetuating. Wilson's Chicago study also found that the daughters of black single mothers are more likely to become single mothers themselves later in life.

Out-of-wedlock births have increased dramatically among all U.S. population groups. The rate of increase among African-Americans has slowed in recent years. But there is little reason to think that African-American families have turned a corner. In a Brookings Institution study (cited by Roland Warren, the president of National Fatherhood Initiative), in the years from 1970 to 2001, the overall marriage rate in the U.S. declined 17 percent, but for blacks it declined 34 percent.

Upon viewing these numbers, some people, especially those sympathetic to the historic and ongoing oppression of African-Americans, are tempted to suggest that perhaps black Americans simply have different family structures and traditions that are just as good as the traditional American two-parent family. Others might hypothesize that the preponderance of out-of-wedlock births and single-parent households among blacks is mainly the result of the high unemployment and incarceration rates afflicting African-American men. And the extremely high incarceration rates of recent years, related to the "war on drugs," certainly could be a factor.

But explanations based on economic hardship don't hold up when we look at the family patterns over a century. According to sociologist Andrew Billingsley, in 1890, among the first generation born after slavery, 80 percent of black families with children were headed by married couples. In 1950, 64 percent of black males aged 16 and older were married compared with 68 percent of comparable white males. By 1998, only 41 percent of adult black males were married. From 1950 to 1998, the percentage of never-married black women doubled. In his article, "Is the American Underclass Growing?", Christopher Jencks notes that "In 1960, 23 percent of black children were born to unwed mothers." Since then the rate has tripled.

These enormous changes in African-American family life have taken place during the very time that overt racial discrimination has begun to subside in America. Certainly no one could claim that black men of 1890, or even 1950, had better prospects than their present-day descendants. So the blame for this problem, which contributes so much to the disproportionate and continuing poverty of African-Americans, cannot be attributed entirely to racial discrimination.

Many historians have noted that while differences in family patterns increased from the 1970s to the 1990s, measurable differences in the makeup of black and white families have existed ever since the first postslavery measurements. It was extremely difficult for slaves to maintain intact families. Even in the best of conditions, where slave couples were able to form marriages, these unions had no legal standing. Owners could and did separate couples from each other and from their children, either by placing them in distant parts of a large plantation or by selling off some members of the family and keeping others. It's only logical that three centuries of such treatment would have lingering effects on the family patterns of subsequent generations. It is also logical that, in the years since 1965, black out-of-wedlock births would have increased in response to a wrong-headed federal welfare policy that said children could only be eligible for public assistance if the father was not in the home. This may not have provided the "incentive" for out-of-wedlock births that conservatives have claimed, but it certainly provided a disincentive for the formation of stable, two-parent families.

In 1999, Gary J. Tschoepe, a professor of political science and public administration at the University of Texas, Pan-Am, published a statistical analysis testing various explanations for African-American out-of-wedlock births. He tested the conservative theories that out-of-wedlock births were encouraged by generous welfare benefits (in what was then the program called Aid to Families with Dependent Children or AFDC) and discouraged by strong traditional moral and religious values. These were tested by comparing states with generous AFDC plans to states with more austere ones and by comparing out-of-wedlock birth rates in Southern states, which are known to be more religious and culturally traditionalist, with those of other regions. He also tested the liberal theory that out-of-wedlock births were encouraged by black male unemployment, which prevented young black fathers from contributing to the support of their families. Finally, he tested the statistical variables of lower male-to-female ratios in the black population of some states and abortion rates (measured as the number of abortions per every one thousand live births in a given state).

Tschoepe found that neither black male unemployment nor generous welfare policies had any measurable impact on the rate of out-of-wedlock births. Out-of-wedlock birth rates did go down slightly in states with higher abortion rates. And male-female population imbalance was a significant factor. Tschoepe noted that public policies aimed at decreasing the mortality rate of black males could, over the long term, have a positive impact on out-of-wedlock birth rates. But the factor that had the most impact was residence in a Southern state. This, Tschoepe wrote, "does provide conservatives with support for their argument that anti-family attitudes have contributed to the problem, and that a transformation of national moral values is necessary."

Ultimately, the choices people make about sexual behavior and family life are personal ones. In the absence of any transforming intervention, they are influenced most heavily by the examples of parents. Out-of-wedlock births and single-parent households have become increasingly common in all ethnic groups and at all income levels. And, as the Tschoepe study suggests, the most likely cause is the transformation of sexual behavior (and divorce law) that began in the late 1960s. Since that time, the individual pursuit of happiness (or simply pleasure) has increasingly replaced the ideal of lifelong commitment to a family. As the bad consequences of this new ethic have mounted, the renewal of sexual responsibility and family solidarity has become an issue for every thoughtful American.

Perhaps because of the legacy of slavery, followed by generations of extreme poverty and lack of education, African-Americans may have proven more vulnerable to the virus of sexual irresponsibility that has infected American culture as a whole. Whatever the cause, no one can deny that a transforming intervention is needed for African-American families. It is equally clear that the initiative for this transformation must come from within the African-American community. More specifically, it is the special responsibility of the historically black Christian churches. Increasingly, African-American clergy and opinion leaders are recognizing the gravity of this problem and trying to start a cultural change. White people of good will can encourage and support such initiatives in ways that are requested.

But it is also clear that no one is helped by denying that single-parent households and out-of-wedlock births are a problem and, at least in part, a problem of individual responsibility. The facts are the facts. On the whole, single-parent families are poorer. On average, the children in them have more problems at school and with the law. And they tend to replicate the pattern for generations to come. Recognizing that the ideal isn't always possible, we must still be able to insist that it is better for children to be raised in a home with two parents who have made a permanent commitment to each other and their children. If anything, it is discriminatory for white people to pretend that for some reason,

African-Americans are somehow not best served by the kind of families we would prefer for our own children.

African-Americans and Criminal Justice

While the problems facing black families suffered from years of well-meaning silence, the issue of African-Americans (especially young black men) and crime has suffered from intentional and misleading overexposure. In the post–civil rights era, the fear of crime provided the perfect cover under which politicians could continue to appeal to the racism of white voters. The demand for "law and order" has often been a code for pandering to white fears of an increasing black presence in a community (Joel Kovel's aversive racism). The image of the violent, black male criminal, so common on local TV news throughout the country, stirs up ghosts of dominative racism that are at least as old as Nat Turner. Under the cover of a "war on drugs," locking up ever-larger numbers of black men for ever-longer periods of time has become a badge of honor for politicians, proving their commitment to protecting America's children.

Crime is the issue where the impact of racism is the most nakedly evident. Due to the lingering influence of the racist mythologies that surrounded the justification of slavery, at a very deep psychological level, many white people expect black men to be savage, violent, and even subhuman. When actual instances of violent behavior by black men are found, they may be seized upon as proof of the racist myth. The news media supply those confirming examples (out of proportion to their real occurrence) because they know that this is what audiences want to see. White audiences, of course, want to see news of black crime because it confirms their deeply held fears. And so the cycle continues.

First, the facts: Do African-Americans, on a per capita basis, commit more crime than white Americans? All the available statistics suggest that they do. In every society on earth, the poorest people are the ones who are most likely to commit street crimes. It's extremely rare for the college-educated son of two lawyers (whatever his race) to rob a liquor store. It's less rare for the son of a single mother who cleans office buildings for minimum wage to commit a robbery. Obviously, most people do not take the risk of crime when they have other, less dangerous, ways to acquire material goods, and equally important, a sense of accomplishment and identity. For the young men of families mired in generations of poverty and bad schooling, who've never seen anyone prosper by working hard and following the rules, crime can seem like a reasonable career path. In a country whose social hierarchy was built on the institution of race-based slavery, a disproportionate number of the young men in those circumstances are also African-American. According to the "Sourcebook of Criminal Justice Statistics" (www.albany.edu/sourcebook), in 2004 roughly 30 percent of the people arrested for crimes were black. African-Americans comprise roughly 13 percent of the U.S. population.

But a report compiled by the Council of Economic Advisors for President Clinton's Initiative on Race contained another set of facts that receives much less public exposure. Blacks are also more likely than whites to be victims of crime. In every category of violent and property crimes, the percentage of black victims exceeded their share of the general population. And the difference was greatest for the most serious crimes. African-Americans are six times more likely to be victims of murder than are white Americans.

All of this confirms the commonsense perception that crime is, to a large extent, a function of poverty. It mostly takes place in the neighborhoods in which the poorest people are concentrated, and it mostly victimizes the people who live in those neighborhoods. So where does the pervasive white middle-class fear of crime in our society come from?

One obvious answer is the news media. According to a report

by Building Blocks for Youth ("Youth, Race & Crime in the News"), some studies have found that local news media depict African-Americans as perpetrators of crime in numbers greater than their actual crime rates. But even in studies that found the number of stories to be roughly proportionate, stories about African-American crime suspects were still longer, less likely to give the suspect's name, and more likely to identify the suspect's race. In addition, blacks are disproportionately depicted as violent. A study of local TV news in Los Angeles found that blacks were 22 percent more likely to appear for committing a violent crime than a nonviolent one, while they were, in reality, equally likely to be arrested for a nonviolent crime. On the other hand, whites were 31 percent more likely to be depicted as committing a nonviolent crime, which they were only 7 percent more likely to have committed.

African-Americans are underreported as crime victims, and white victims are overreported. White murder victims, especially, are three times more likely to receive news coverage than are African-American victims (who outnumber them six times over). Interracial crimes were found to be among the most over-reported. For example, one study of local TV news in Philadelphia found that four out of ten stories about black murder suspects depicted a crime against a white victim, while in reality only one out of ten murders was black-on-white.

When we look at the whole picture this report presents, we see black people being depicted as the perpetrators of crime and white people as the crime victims. The failure to adequately report black victimization leaves white audiences with the false impression that crime in America is mostly a matter of black people robbing, attacking, and killing white people. It should then be no surprise that public opinion polling has shown that white Americans overestimate, by a margin of three to one, their likelihood of being the victim of a black criminal.

In the real world of American criminal justice, the Leadership

Conference on Civil Rights (LCCR), a coalition of the leading national civil rights organizations, has found that African-Americans receive discriminatory treatment at every stage of the process, from investigation to arrest to trial, sentencing, and incarceration.

Blacks are disproportionately targeted as suspects, the LCCR report says. Traffic stops on Interstate 95 in the state of Maryland were monitored from 1995 to 1997 as part of a federal court judgment on racial profiling. The monitors found that 70 percent of the motorists stopped on the highway were black, while blacks made up only 17 percent of the motorists (and speeders). In central Florida it was found that 70 percent of the people stopped on one stretch of interstate were black or Hispanic, but blacks and Hispanics were only 5 percent of the total drivers.

Disproportionate targeting inevitably leads to disproportionate arrest. Once arrested, black defendants were found to face disparate treatment in plea bargaining and sentencing. A study of the California courts by the *San Jose Mercury News* found that blacks were less likely than whites to have their charges dismissed or reduced to a misdemeanor and less likely to receive alternative sentencing rather than incarceration.

A New York state government study found that blacks are more likely to go to prison than whites who have committed the same crimes. One-third of the blacks and Hispanics sentenced to prison in New York would have received lighter sentences if they had been treated like white defendants charged with the same crime and holding the same criminal record. If blacks had received probation at the same rate as their white counterparts, more than 8,000 fewer black defendants would have gone to state prison in the two-year period studied. This would have meant a 5five percent decline in the percentage of blacks among the inmates sentenced in those years.

Perhaps the worst examples of criminal justice discrimination resulted from the "drug war" that began with the arrival of crack cocaine in the mid-1980s. The Leadership Conference noted that "From 1986 to 1991, arrests of white juveniles for drug offenses *decreased* [emphasis added] 34 percent, while arrests of minority juveniles increased 78 percent." This was despite surveys showing that drug use rates among white, black, and Hispanic youths are roughly equal.

The U.S.-based organization Human Rights Watch has identified the disproportionate incarceration of African-Americans as an international human rights violation. According to Human Rights Watch:

> Blacks comprise 13 percent of the national population, but 30 percent of people arrested, 41 percent of people in jail, and 49 percent of those in prison. Nine percent of all black adults are under some form of correctional supervision (in jail or prison, on probation or parole), compared to two percent of white adults. One in three black men between the ages of 20 and 29 was either in jail or prison, or on parole or probation in 1995. One in ten black men in their twenties and early thirties is in prison or jail. Thirteen percent of the black adult male population has lost the right to vote because of felony disenfranchisement laws.

The ripple effects of this treatment of black men in the criminal justice system are staggering. Prison records follow men throughout their entire life, making employment difficult and thus making future offenses more likely. Every black man in prison represents a lost father or uncle in a black family. For this reason alone, discrimination by the police and courts is an issue of justice that should concern the entire community wherever it takes place, and the evidence suggests that it takes place almost everywhere.

Chapter 10

Racial Remedies? Affirmative Action and Reparations

We've seen that most of America's racial injustices are rooted in the past—especially in the horror of slavery and the systematic dehumanization of Jim Crow. Given those facts, logic would suggest that any attempt to establish justice might go beyond simply acknowledging that past and actually try to make some form of restitution for it.

That was the logic President Lyndon Johnson was following when he instituted the first affirmative action programs in the federal government in 1965. Johnson saw that civil rights legislation had removed many of the legal barriers to black equality. It had put all Americans at the same starting line in life. But as a Southerner, Johnson also knew very well that African-Americans began the race of life under a heavy weight of inherited disadvantages. They had been denied all access to education for centuries and then deliberately consigned to inferior schools and excluded from the higher-paying jobs for several decades. In addition, despite the laws against overt discrimination, Johnson knew that blacks would still face the disadvantage of widespread and deeply rooted racial prejudice among large numbers of white people.

Johnson and his civil rights advisors believed that to achieve real equality under the weight of all this baggage, African-Americans would need a head start. Affirmative action was intended to provide a systematic way to account for the historic damage done to African-Americans and to give them a chance to move forward less encumbered by that past.

The first affirmative action programs involved hiring for federal jobs and in companies doing business with the federal government. In the four decades since, affirmative action has spread into many areas of American life, most notably the admission process at many colleges and professional schools, the letting of contracts with private businesses by many state and local governments, and employment in many agencies (such as law enforcement) and occupations (such as skilled construction trades) where courts have found a history of discrimination.

Affirmative action was always expected to be a temporary remedy. As it has spread and continued, questions have periodically arisen about its efficacy and its justice.

One criticism of the efficacy of race-based affirmative action is that it mostly benefits middle-class African-Americans who are prepared to take advantage of the opportunities affirmative action creates, but does very little for the poorest African-Americans, who are presumably the ones most damaged by the legacy of slavery and discrimination.

Randall Robinson, the founder of TransAfrica and mastermind of the U.S. Free South Africa movement in the 1980s, stated this point well in his book, *The Debt: What America Owes to Blacks.* Affirmative action programs, Robinson said:

> . . . are palliatives that help people like me, who are poised to succeed when given half a chance. They do little for the millions of African-Americans bottom-mired in urban hells by the savage time-release social debilitations of American slavery. They do little for those . . . who inherit grinding poverty, poor nutrition, bad schools, unsafe neighborhoods, low expectation, and overburdened mothers.

When Derek Bok and William Bowen, the former presidents of Harvard and Princeton respectively, conducted a study of admissions at twenty-eight elite universities, they found evidence to support Robinson's claim. They discovered that 86 percent of the African-American students at those institutions came from middle- or upper-middle-class families. In the same way, minority set-asides in government contracting have helped create and expand the class of black entrepreneurs in many urban areas. But they have done nothing to raise the stagnant wages of ordinary blue-collar workers.

Questions about the efficacy of affirmative action go hand-in-hand with legitimate questions about the justice of granting favorable treatment solely on the basis of race. Many conservatives, especially, never tire of quoting Martin Luther King, Jr.'s dream of a day when people are judged by the "content of their character" rather than the color of their skin. On the surface, affirmative action, which explicitly considers the color of a school or job applicant's skin, seems to contradict that dream. Furthermore, critics argue, where is the justice in a program that, for instance, gives preference for college admission to the child of a wealthy black doctor or corporate executive over a young white person who may have grown up living on minimum wage and food stamps in a rented trailer?

Much of the affirmative action debate, including the most important court cases, has come to revolve around admission to the most selective colleges and universities. This is because today more than ever, those institutions are the gateway through which people enter America's professional elite. If black students can attain parity in these schools, the argument goes, a critical mass of black professionals will get their hands on the levers of power, and discrimination will begin to fade away. Some critics have suggested that in college admissions, that goal can be accomplished without the perceived injustice of favoring rich blacks over poor whites. This could be done, the critics say, by using a class-based system that considers household income and family history instead of race.

Supporters of race-based affirmative action reply that, again focusing on college admissions, the race gap in standardized test scores (see chapter 1) means that class-based affirmative action would still end up meaning fewer black students in the elite schools.

The argument is further complicated by the fact that redress of past wrongs is no longer the main justification put forward for affirmative action in higher education. In the University of Michigan case of 2004, the Supreme Court recognized the validity of affirmative action used to further the value of diversity in the educational process.

This argument is highly favored by U.S.-based global corporations, many of whom filed friend-of-the-court briefs in support of affirmative action in the Michigan case. Corporate America supports affirmative action for diversity because young executives from various racial backgrounds help open doors for American companies in the nonwhite world. But the use of affirmative action to foster an atmosphere of ethnic and cultural diversity would also make what began as a temporary remedy into a permanent fact of American life. We may want to give racial distinctions a permanent place in the workings of our society as a way of both establishing racial justice and managing the multiracial American future. But we should certainly be aware that we are doing it and give serious thought to the consequences.

Author, philosopher, and activist Cornel West, in his landmark book, *Race Matters*, says that he favors class-based affirmative action "in principle." He also acknowledges that affirmative action as practiced today mostly benefits the black middle class. Still, he says of race-based affirmative action, "[It] is not the most important issue for black progress in America, but it is part of a redistributive chain that must be strengthened if we are to confront and eliminate black poverty."

Forty Acres and a Mule

When Civil War General William Tecumseh Sherman made his infamous march to the Georgia sea coast, all along the way he burned plantation houses and freed plantation slaves, in keeping with President Lincoln's Emancipation Proclamation. Upon reaching the coast, he issued a field command that every freed slave be provided with a forty-acre plot of former plantation land and the loan of a government mule. This, he thought, would be sufficient to insure the survival and independence of the former slaves in years to come.

Eventually, higher-ups in Washington, D.C. vetoed this order and forced Sherman to rescind it, but the idea never went away. Almost 150 years later, "forty acres and a mule" still serves as a catch phrase for the just recompense that the former slaves never received. In recent years, the idea that America should make some kind of formal, material reparations to the descendants of slaves has become more widely discussed than at any time since Sherman's day.

Support for some form of reparations for slavery has begun to build in response to other instances in which governments have made cash payments for past atrocities or abuses. The German government has paid reparations to Holocaust survivors and to the state of Israel. More recently, concentration camp survivors and their descendants have been awarded money from German corporations that profited from Jewish slave labor. In 1988, the U.S. government made a formal apology and a cash payment of $20,000 to every Japanese-American who was imprisoned without cause during World War II. Some Native American nations have accepted cash payments in compensation for land taken illegally.

Developments in class-action litigation, such as the massive, successful lawsuit by the states against the tobacco industry, have also encouraged leading legal scholars to look at the possibility of reparations lawsuits, especially against still-existing companies that profited from slavery. Already, reparations have been granted for some specific incidents of racist violence against blacks. The state of Florida has paid out $2.1 million to descendants of the victims of racist attacks in a riot at Rosewood, Florida in 1923. The city of Tulsa, Oklahoma is considering similar payment in compensation for a 1921 riot in which as many as 300 African-Americans were killed.

Many reparations advocates hope that the truth commission proposed by Rep. John Conyers will lay the investigative groundwork to recommend a reparations policy. As law professor Art Alcausin Hall has put it, "You don't simply say 'I'm sorry' to a man you've robbed.... You return what you stole or your apology takes on a hollow ring."

There is a wide variety of ideas about how to make reparations. Some advocates favor individual cash payments to the poorest African-Americans, as well as the establishment of permanent education funds and perhaps a pool of money for low-interest business loans to be available exclusively to the descendants of slaves. Randall Robinson, whose book, *The Debt*, has helped put reparations on the public agenda, says, "I'm not calling for reparations paid directly in cash amounts to people. I'm saying we ought to establish government-funded programs and trusts that would fund education and economic development in the black community, until these gaps are closed, until we have an equal America." This is necessary, Robinson adds, because, "In a legal and moral sense, we have to atone as a society and make this enormous wrong right."

Professor Charles Ogletree at Harvard Law School is leading a group of lawyers who are looking for ways to get the reparations issue into court. Without venturing into proposing specific remedies, Ogletree has stated that a reparations program should embody four primary features: "(1) a focus on the past to account for the present; (2) a focus on the present, to reveal the continuing existence of race-based discrimination; (3) an accounting of the past harms or injuries that have not been compensated; and (4) a challenge to society to devise ways to respond as a whole to the uncompensated harms identified in the past."

Wendy Kaminer, a white liberal attorney and resident scholar at Radcliffe College, sees problems with even identifying who should receive reparations. She says, "I would have supported reparations for slavery in the generation or two after slavery ended, because you could identify the actual victims of slavery, you could identify their children, but you can't do that anymore, and it gets so complicated in this country when so many Americans are mixed-race people, so many African-Americans are mixed-race, they have white ancestors, they have ancestors who were slaveholders, as well as ancestors who were slaves." In addition, Kaminer is concerned with the moral framework a debate about reparations would establish for American racial politics. "The way reparations are presented and perceived," she says, "encourages this sense of inherited guilt, and also a sense that you somehow inherit virtue through the oppression of your ancestors, and I think that those are both very destructive notions."

Glenn Loury, an African-American economist and director of the Institute on Race and Social Division at Boston University, believes that no amount of money could compensate for the damage of slavery. He told the *New York Times*, "We need some reckoning with the racist past, but reparations encourage the wrong kind of reckoning. . . . As in South Africa, the deepest and most relevant 'reparation' would entail constructing and inculcating in our citizens an account of how we have come to be as we are—one that avoids putting the responsibility for the current problems of African-Americans wholly on their shoulders."

Adolf Reed is an African-American professor of political science at the New School in New York City. He suggests that the campaign for reparations is a political dead end. He questions the tactical wisdom of asking people to "mobilize around earlier generations' grievances to pursue current objectives." And worse, Reed believes that a campaign for reparations could destroy opportunities for real progress that would benefit a broad majority of low- and moderate-income Americans, black, white, and brown. Reed wrote in *The Progressive:*

> We are in one of those rare moments in American history—like the 1880s and 1890s and the Great Depression—when common circumstances of economic and social insecurity have strengthened the potential for building broad solidarity across race, gender, and other identities around shared concerns of daily life. . . . These are concerns that . . . can be pursued effectively only by struggling to unite a wide section of the American population that is denied those essential social benefits or lives in fear of losing them. Isn't it interesting that at such a moment the corporate-dominated, opinion-shaping media discover and project a demand for racially defined reparations that cuts precisely against building such solidarity?

And there lies the crux of the reparations debate. If we use the recommendations of the Vatican commission as our guide, a faithful response to race in America should include an acknowledgment of past crimes and sins, penitent attempts to right those wrongs, and measures aimed at promoting the solidarity of people across racial lines. There can be no denying that a program of reparations to African-American descendants of slaves, if such could be practically arranged, would accomplish those first two goals. But could it be done in a way that brings people together, rather than deepening divisive resentments and fears?

Chapter 11

What Next? Building Solidarity

Ultimately, when it comes to addressing racism, the Christian goal is to restore the unity that God intends among His people. History, economics, and psychology complicate the task. But our study of the historical roots of racism and analysis of contemporary power relations are intended to help us understand the sources and causes of our divisions so that we can overcome them. When we are ready to go into action, we should begin with actions that forge or strengthen the bonds of human solidarity across racial lines, first among Christians, and then in the broader community.

Interracial solidarity begins locally, with face-to-face relationships between people of different races who are honestly trying to be reconciled and united, and are willing to do the hard things that may require. The process of building solidarity will be different in every community. There is no magic formula. But the following examples, one from a big northern city and another from a small southern town, can at least provide a starting place for thinking as Catholic Christians about our local response to racism. It's worth noting that both of these stories begin with a violent racial crisis. But we don't have to wait for bloodshed to attack the roots of racial division.

A New Wind in Chicago

When he called Chicago the "city with big shoulders" and the "hog butcher to the world," poet Carl Sandburg captured some of the ways in which the city on Lake Michigan embodies America's hard-working, down-to-earth virtues. Unfortunately the city, which has also been called "America's most segregated," has an equally strong dose of America's greatest vice. Ever since African-American migrants from the South began arriving in the city during World War I, Chicago's European ethnic communities have struggled with how, or whether, to accommodate them. In 1966, Chicago was the scene of Martin Luther King, Jr.'s greatest defeat, as violent mobs and city hall resistance turned back his attempts to bring the civil rights movement to the North.

In the 1980s, the city's first African-American mayor, Harold Washington, was elected when he combined the votes of blacks, Hispanics, and white reformers. But Washington's promise of equal power-sharing among the city's communities was cut short by his early death from a heart attack.

Today, under the leadership of Cardinal Francis George, the Catholic Church is making a new effort to help lead the city beyond its legacy of racism. When George came to Chicago as cardinal in 1997, he immediately faced a boiling racial crisis. On the first day of spring that year, two African-American boys, thirteen-year-old Lenard Clark and his friend, Clevan Nicholson, were riding bicycles home from a basketball game. Their route took them along the edge of the Bridgeport neighborhood, which had been home to the late Mayor Richard Daley and a center of violent resistance to racial integration. Along the way, three white male teenagers stopped the two black youths and knocked them off their bikes. Lenard Clark tried to run away, and the three white boys chased him down and viciously beat and kicked him until he was left in a coma. There had been no provocation by the two black boys, no misinterpreted insult or other excuse. Lenard

Clark was beaten nearly to death solely because he was black. Many whites were shocked that this kind of overt racist violence could still take place in their city, and African-American Chicagoans were enraged.

The story of Lenard Clark spread around the world via television. That weekend, in his weekly radio address, President Clinton talked about the attack on Lenard Clark and the scourge of racism that still afflicted the country. Eventually, Clevan Nicholson, who was less severely injured than Clark, was able to identify the three white attackers. Two of them pleaded guilty and received probation; the third stood trial and was sentenced to eight years in prison. The new cardinal, in response, vowed to lead his archdiocese into the new millennium "free from the sin of racism."

Cardinal George began a process of consultation with the archdiocesan task force on racial justice that culminated with *Dwell in My Love: A Pastoral Letter on Racism*, released on April 4, 2001, the anniversary of the assassination of Martin Luther King.

In that letter, the cardinal proclaimed that "racism contradicts God's will for our salvation; we can not claim to love God without loving our neighbor" and noted, "It's not just a question of justice for some folks, it's a question of freedom for all. People who are racist are trapped, not free."

But it was the quotation on the title page that carried the letter's deepest message, "We are called," the cardinal told his flock, "not only to a radical conversion of heart but to a transformation of socially sinful structures as well."

The pastoral letter analyzed four types of racism: "spatial, institutional, internalized and individual." Spatial racism referred to the patterns of residential segregation that mark all American cities, but are especially powerful in Chicago. These patterns, he noted, also lead to segregated Catholic parishes. Institutional racism referred to the bias embedded in social structures that works against people of color. Internalized racism referred to the effect of racism upon some of its victims, who absorb lifelong messages of inferiority; and individual racism referred to personal prejudice. *Dwell in My Love* ended with a series of recommended antiracist actions for the archdiocese, its parishes and its schools.

What set *Dwell in My Love* apart from many other well-meaning and well-wrought statements by church leaders of various denominations through the years was the fact that the Archdiocese of Chicago put resources and action behind the letter's fine sentiments. Rather than keeping antiracist work on the laundry list of tasks assigned to the Office of Justice and Peace, George established an Archdiocesan Office of Racial Justice devoted solely to implementing the directives of *Dwell in My Love*. Next he appointed his own executive assistant, Anita George, an African-American sister of the Daughters of the Holy Heart of Mary, to head it.

Today the Office of Racial Justice represents a viable model of how a multiethnic, but predominantly white, faith community can begin taking steps to free itself from what the cardinal called "the sin of racism."

First, the archdiocesan leadership team was trained by an organization specializing in antiracist education. The training was designed to develop an understanding of the roots of racism, a common analysis of institutional racism, and an ability to identify the subtle ways that racial stereotypes often function to benefit whites and penalize people of color. Next, the training was spread to the entire archdiocesan staff and the staff of the parishes and schools and was offered to the people in the pews. The Office on Racial Justice began offering three levels or phases of "Workshops on Racism and Ethnic Sensitivity."

In the first five years of the office's existence, about 3,000 people from more than three hundred parishes participated in workshops on racism. Already, the new understandings born in these workshops have issued forth in new actions. After participating

in the workshops, members of three parishes—one predominantly black, one Latino, and one suburban and predominantly
white—banded together to form Catholics Against Racism
(CAR), with the slogan, "We need more drivers." Later they were
joined by members of another predominantly white parish. The
purpose of the organization is "to make people aware that the sin
of racism is prevalent in our hearts, our neighborhoods, our society and its institutions." The group has carried its message
through activities such as marching in parades for Columbus Day
and the Fourth of July with antiracist banners and testifying in
public hearings on behalf of more funding for public schools.

Meanwhile, students and faculty at a dozen Chicago-area
Catholic high schools have formed Catholic Schools Opposing
Racism (COR). COR carries out diversity workshops in the
schools and uses visual arts, music, storytelling, and theater to
address issues of racism. Several times a year, COR also sponsors
rallies and concerts and provides other occasions for students to
meet each other and work together across the boundaries of their
segregated neighborhood.

Recognizing that Chicago's racial divisions, like America's,
are no longer simple matters of black and white, the Office on
Racial Justice has begun offering its workshops in Spanish, with
the content adapted to make sense of the different experiences of
racism that Latinos bring from their native countries, as well as
the U.S. racial dynamics into which they have come. The Office
of Racial Justice has also helped two neighboring parishes, one
black and one Latino, to address "racial tension and fear" between
the two communities. Together the parishes have organized a
"Peace and Unity Walk" culminating in a Unity Mass. According
the Office of Racial Justice newsletter, "Together, as Children of
God, those present learned of the rich spiritual and cultural gifts
each community possesses and the gifts they have in common."

On a citywide level, the Office of Racial Justice sponsors an
annual "Unity Rally and a Racial Justice Week" around the January

birthday of Martin Luther King. Chicago still has plenty of problems, but at least its Catholic Christians are becoming more aware of those problems. And that awareness creates the opportunity for the wind of the Spirit to blow.

Diversity in Decatur

At the Oakhurst Presbyterian Church, there's a black Jesus in front, a white Jesus in back and folks of both colors in between. The black Jesus depicted on a stained-glass window in front used to be white, but the pastor of Oakhurst, the Rev. Gibson Stroupe, and his wife Caroline Leach tinted the once pink portrait brown. Both Leach and Stroupe are white, and she admits "we did get some flak" for the racial alteration. . . . Some chose to leave the church and the neighborhood, looking for greener pastures and whiter places in which to live and worship. And then there were those that came, saw and stayed. In a perfect world, religion should be color-blind. Oakhurst isn't in that perfect world. It's in Decatur, Georgia. (Christopher John Farley, in *Time* magazine.)

Decatur, Georgia was once a small town. Then, a short distance down the road, someone started a place called Atlanta. Decatur has been a suburb for a long time now. In the 1960s, it was a very prosperous, and almost all-white, suburb. In those days Oakhurst Presbyterian Church was prosperous, too, with nine hundred members, all of them white.

What happened next at Oakhurst has happened to hundreds, maybe thousands, of congregations and neighborhoods all over the U.S. in the past fifty years. A few black families moved into the area, and soon almost all the white families moved out. By 1983, Oakhurst Presbyterian was down to eighty members. Most were whites who traveled back to the old neighborhood on Sunday; a few were black newcomers to Decatur.

In most cases, this story would end with the church closing or relocating to a more distant suburb and selling the building to an African-American congregation. But something different happened at Oakhurst. Today it is a growing congregation of about two hundred, half black and half white, that calls itself "Multicultural, Forward-Thinking, Jesus-Centered and Biblically-Based." According to Gibson "Nibs" Stroupe, who became pastor of Oakhurst in 1983, "The long journey to health [began] with one giant step: white people and black people deciding to stay in the presence of one another."

In their book, *While We Run This Race*, Stroupe and African-American church elder Inez Fleming recount some of the early difficulties that big decision brought.

One bump in the road came early in Stroupe's tenure when the church's white music director resigned. The search committee to find a replacement recommended a black man, a brilliant musician who had just left a job at a prestigious white church. Ten of the church's twelve elders—six white and four black—were present at the meeting that decided the issue. Despite the man's "impeccable credentials," Stroupe recalls, the vote tied five to five. One white elder supported the hire; all the rest lined up against it. As pastor, Stroupe exercised his prerogative to break the tie. "It was," Stroupe says, "a lesson in the vision of diversity and the reality of racism. There was also irony in this decision. . . . None of us got exactly what we had voted for. Our first African-American music director did not like gospel music. . . . It was as if God was laughing at us."

In 1986, Inez Fleming had married an African-American member of Oakhurst. "I came over," she says, "with the intention of winning my husband back to my church, the black church. I could not believe that any self-respecting African-American would be part of a church with a lot of white folks and especially with a white man as a pastor." However, Fleming was surprised at what she found. "There actually seemed to be some white folks there who genuinely wanted to learn about their own racism and about my people. . . . I also heard . . . that I didn't always have to be 'nice' . . . that it was not only permissible to acknowledge the power of racism in this diverse community of faith—it was an absolute necessity, part of the faith journey."

As she settled in at Oakhurst Church, Fleming says she began to feel the need for the support of a "black women's group" within the church. She brought the proposal of a support group for African-American women to the congregation's governing body and a storm ensued. "The problem that we encountered," Fleming writes, ". . . was our own self-image. We are a multiracial church, and part of our image as Oakhurst is a wonderful community where everyone gets along."

Some white members of the council said that endorsing a separate group for black women amounted to endorsing "the system of race" that the congregation had vowed to resist. A black member insisted that view was "not realistic."

"During this discussion," Fleming recalls, "Nibs, my pastor and my friend, disappointed me." As moderator of the meeting, she says, Stroupe subtly steered the group toward a compromise in which the black women's group would be allowed to meet in the church building but not be officially recognized as an activity of the church. "Most of the elders seemed agreeable to this until it came to me," Fleming says. "I would not accept it." At that point, she recounts, Stroupe recognized what he had done and apologized, and a vote was held on the original motion.

The elders did endorse the black women's group. But Fleming remembers that even that victory was bittersweet. The turning point came when "a white sister spoke in support of the proposal, saying that she understood the objections and the seeming contradiction but felt that we ought to listen to the reality." As Fleming puts it, the good news was that a white woman heard the black women's concerns, trusted them, and stepped outside her comfort zone to support them. The bad news, however, was that it took the voice of a white woman to carry the day.

In the course of forging a multiracial Christian community at Oakhurst Presbyterian Church, whites have had to learn not to be the bosses. And blacks have had to learn not be silent, but to risk confronting white people about their racism. Both lessons have been difficult, but the results have been truly redemptive.

The foundation of Oakhurst's communal life, Stroupe says, is the belief that "God is our central definition. . . . We are defined, first and foremost as children of God." Stroupe tells a story of a black grandmother in his congregation who was concerned that life in the Oakhurst community had made her five-year-old granddaughter "too comfortable around white people." One day grandmother and granddaughter were in a crowded shopping mall. A white man accidentally bumped the little black girl and moved on without a word. The girl turned to him and said, "You forgot to say, 'excuse me.'" The man kept walking, and the little girl ran to overtake him and repeat her admonition. Finally, the white man apologized.

This little girl was growing up in an environment in which black and white people viewed each other as human beings, "and now she expected all white people to receive her as a human being." At some point in the girl's future, her grandmother feared, things might not end that politely. But the grandmother and Stroupe agreed that this was a far better starting place for a child, and she would have the support she needed to face harsh realities when they came.

Since the members' identity as children of God is central to Oakhurst's mission, affirming that identity in worship has been central to building a truly diverse and inclusive faith community. The gospel choir has played a large role in this, but so has a time for "Sharing of Joys and Concerns" in which members bring before the community the trials and triumphs of their week. This sharing draws the community together and shows people of different races how similar their concerns really are—especially when they involve children and family. Oakhurst Presbyterian's life as a diverse congregation has also borne fruit in a diversity of ministries. The church offers "Combating Racism" workshops, participates in community hunger and AIDS projects, and works with prisoners.

Talking and Walking

While the circumstances are different, these two examples have certain common threads which are shared by most other experiences of improved interracial solidarity. They are honest dialogue and sharing of experiences, shared worship and prayer, and shared action.

As we've seen, we must begin by acknowledging the existence of racism and the different ways that we, people of all races, are affected by it. This process allows us to expand our empathy and, usually for the first time, see the world through the eyes of the members of another race.

But talk can also become circular or self-involved. We all need to place our differences and our personal experiences in the larger context of our common ground as children of God. We need to use the gifts of our different traditions of prayer and worship to join together in acknowledging God as our Creator and seeking God's Spirit of love to transform our visions of one another and our relationships.

As St. James rather sternly informed us, "Faith without works is dead." Common understanding and shared worship, if they are real, should lead to shared work ministering with the poor, sick, or imprisoned, and working for justice in the civic community.

One of the most powerful experiences of interracial solidarity in my own experience came when my very small Catholic parish in north Mississippi, in response to a call from our bishop, announced in the local paper that we would hold a prayer vigil on the evening that a death-row inmate was scheduled to be executed. It was the first execution in the state after several years of legal delay, and the man slated for execution was white.

Our vigil was held at the Catholic Church. Most of our very small English-speaking (mostly white) congregation showed up, and a fair sampling of the Hispanics. We were joined by a few kindred spirits from white mainline Protestant congregations. Then, just as the service was about to begin, the pastor and his family and the entire youth choir from a neighboring black Baptist church walked in unexpectedly to join us in repenting for our part in the inmate's death and to pray for the soul of this white man and his white victim, a state policeman. Prayers and songs from the African-American Christian tradition transformed our gathering, and the shared witness for life and justice created a new set of relationships. None of it would have happened if our congregation had been afraid to take what was, in our community, a very unpopular public stand.

Daily Steps against Racism

The stories cited so far are all examples in which church and shared faith serve as the vehicle for racial reconciliation. And that is a central task of any congregation in America today. But as central as the faith community may be to our lives, most of us spend most of our time in the worlds of work and family life. And, for most of us, our most important and time-consuming project is the rearing of children who, in turn, spend most of their time in schools.

It is in this long march of daily existence that we show what is truly important to us. If we are going to make it a priority to become white people who are part of the solution to racism, we will do it mostly in our daily lives as workers and family members.

If we live in a racially-mixed area or work in a diverse environment, many of the daily steps are obvious. We reach out to our black neighbors and coworkers. We don't always sit next to the people we already know (who are probably white) at lunches or meetings. We speak up about any racially-offensive language or imagery that might turn up in the shared environment. It is especially important that black people not have to take the initiative to correct whites who act in discriminatory or offensive ways. That should be our job. If we are in a position of responsibility, we always try to make sure that African-Americans have a chance to take leadership positions, and we initiate honest, open and intentional conversations among neighbors or coworkers about the racial environment and our various perceptions of it.

But the sad facts are that most white Americans live lives in which they rarely encounter real black people. We are separated not only by race, but often by income and class and by urban geography shaped by economics and race. Some of us may live in places—say in upper New England or the mountain West or much of the Great Plains—where there are still very few minority residents at all. In these cases, we must be even more intentional about our antiracist practices, because in the absence of real African-Americans, perceptions are formed by the mass media, which, as we've seen, are unreliable messengers.

In these cases, we can take some of the following suggestions, which are offered not as an exhaustive program, but simply as a few good places to start:

1. Be advocates for equality.
We must speak out whenever we hear a racial slur or stereotype presented. This is often uncomfortable. Today we are likely to be accused of empty-headed "political correctness." But these things matter. It is a simple matter of human decency that all people be granted basic respect, and we can't compromise on this, anywhere. Explain to those around you the significance of issues such

as affirmative action, race, and crime and African-American family life that so often receive, at best, one-dimensional treatment in the media.

2. Become informed about other people's worlds.
Black history, for instance, is not just for Black History Month, and it's not just for black people. It is American history, and if we don't know it, we don't know our own country. We should read books such as Taylor Branch's three-part biography of Martin Luther King, *The Autobiography of Malcolm X,* and the books written by King. We should take in the work of black artists, such as the films of Spike Lee, the novels and memoirs of John Edgar Wideman, or the poetry of Rita Dove—simply because they are among America's most important artists. If we Web-surf for news and views of the world, we shouldn't just check out MSNBC or CNN, or even Slate and Salon; we should venture over to blackcommentator.com and AOL Black Voices (formerly Africana.com). If possible, either locally or when traveling, take the opportunity to worship at a predominantly African-American congregation. Don't worry; you will be welcomed.

3. Make race part of our childrearing.
We can make sure that our children have books and videos and toys that expose them to the full range of American humanity *and* to the reality of racism, past and present. As involved parents, we should make sure that those realities are reflected in the curriculum, materials, and seasonal programs at our children's schools. When we go on family vacations, we should incorporate tourist sites and museums related to African-American history and culture. You will have to go out of your way to ask questions and look for these. But you will find them almost anywhere that there is a significant African-American population.

Chapter 12

Rising to Common Ground

As we've seen, American white racism arose, beginning in the 1600s, to justify and support the American slave system. The turn toward African slave labor on the Virginia plantations in the later seventeenth century was accompanied by the invention of codes and customs to place people of African descent in a separate, somewhat less than human, category. And, as we saw, this happened partly in response to the threat, made real in Bacon's Rebellion, that African servants and slaves might unite with white indentured servants and former servants to overthrow the power of the colony's large landowners.

Over the centuries of slavery, the ideology of white racism grew and took on a life of its own far beyond its original economic purpose. But that economic purpose still lies beneath it. When the slave system ended in 1865, it again became possible for black and poor white workers and farmers to discover their common economic interests and make common cause against the power of wealth. And, for a brief time, during the populist movement of the 1880s, they did this. As Southern historian C. Vann Woodward told us, "Never before or since have the two races in the South come so close together as they did during the Populist struggle." The Jim Crow system of rigid racial separation and inequality was instituted, at least in part, to avert the threat represented by the populist rebellion.

As African political scientist Adolf Reed noted in his discussion of the reparations issue, it has always been in the interest of America's economic elite to assert the supremacy of race over class, to say that differences in color are more important than our common humanity and common interests. The racial divisions that have become so real and run so deeply in our culture have their roots in a strategy to divide the working people of the country by color in order to contain their aspirations for economic equality.

Adolf Reed suggests that today, "We are in one of those rare moments in American history—like the 1880s and 1890s and the Great Depression—when common circumstances of economic and social insecurity have strengthened the potential for building broad solidarity across race, gender, and other identities around shared concerns of daily life."

This is true because since 1973, the average wage for hourly workers in America has been mostly stagnant or declining. The decline halted for a time during the 1990s but has resumed in every year since 2001. This has happened because the higher-paying manufacturing jobs that were the basis of America's broad middle-class prosperity in the 1950s and 1960s have, in large part, been shipped offshore and replaced by lower-paying service and retail jobs. The downward pressure on wages has been exacerbated by congressional refusal to raise the minimum wage, by employers' use of the undocumented immigrant work force, and by developments in labor law that have made union organization more difficult.

Our postindustrial information economy is becoming almost as stratified as the plantation system of the early nineteenth century. The upper fifth of the country, college-educated and highly skilled, has seen its income take off like a rocket, while the bottom 40 percent have been in decline, and those in between are treading water. The information economy is a bonanza for software designers, copyright lawyers, and advertising executives.

But it's not so great for the people who move boxes at the Amazon warehouse or work the cash register at Best Buy.

The loss of blue-collar jobs that pay an adequate salary has been especially brutal for African-Americans. In the early 1970s, just as the mass of African-American people had gained their rights and were prepared to begin climbing the American ladder of success, the global economy pulled the lower rungs off the ladder. This is an important factor in the persistent income and employment gaps between black and white Americans.

But these new economic realities have been devastating for all lower-income American workers, regardless of race. Declining wages have not shown up as strongly in household income statistics. This reflects the fact that most American households have clung to middle-class status by sending more family members into the paid work force, working more overtime, and amassing incredible levels of credit card debt. So far, the costs of declining wages have been pushed off onto family life and borne in the form of marital stress, bad diet, unattended children, and, finally, bankruptcy.

Most Americans do not have college degrees, and most Americans have not benefited from the free-trade global economy. The broad majority of black and white Americans, and many Hispanics as well, are now, more than ever, in the same boat. They have powerful common interests in seeing better public schools that will help their children cope with the information age, health care policies that will guarantee affordable access— especially for parents who stay out of the full-time work-force, and trade and investment policies that will encourage the growth of higher-wage manufacturing jobs on American soil.

They have these common interests. But they are divided by the illusions of racial stereotypes and culture wars. As it was in the day of Bacon's rebellion, real racial reconciliation in America today would quickly become a threat to the economic status quo. What Tom Watson said 120 years ago is still true of most black, white, and brown Americans: "You are kept apart so that you may be separately fleeced of your earnings. You are made to hate each other because upon that hatred is rested the keystone of the arch of financial despotism which enslaves you both."

But how, in our distracted, multi-tasked twenty-first century world, are people of different races going to find each other and discover their common interests? In the 1880s, the vehicle for the interracial coalition was the local populist-organized farm cooperative. In the 1930s, it was the labor union. Today less than a tenth of private-sector workers belong to unions, and low and moderate income people are dispersed into subdivisions living two-job lives in which they only see their neighbors in the driveway.

There is, however, one place where most Americans still, on a regular basis, sit down with other members of their community and contemplate deep questions of meaning and values. That is in their religious congregations. The vast majority of Americans no longer have labor unions; they don't have time for neighborhood associations; even PTA participation is in decline; but Americans still go to the church, synagogue, or mosque. That is where the old hope for America's multiracial democracy can still be found.

But, you wonder, isn't it still true that as Martin Luther King once said, 11:00 Sunday morning is the most racially-segregated hour of the week?

It's less true than it was fifty years ago, but churches are still mostly separated by race. In the past twenty-five years, however, a new breed of community organizers has devised a practical and powerful model for community action that brings religious people together across lines of race, denomination, income, and urban-suburban geography.

Common Values and Common Interests

It all began in the late 1970s in the Industrial Areas Foundation (IAF). IAF was the community organizing network founded by

Saul Alinsky, who from the 1930s to the 1960s succeeded in building organizations to empower low-income communities in urban neighborhoods across the country, often with the support of Catholic diocesan agencies. But by the 1970s, the limitations of the "turf-based" neighborhood organizing approach had become obvious. Urban renewal, the construction of interstate highways, and the decline of manufacturing industries had dispersed the old IAF constituencies into postindustrial suburbs without geographic or cultural centers. People who tried to build neighborhood organizations increasingly found themselves spending most of their time introducing neighbors to each other.

That's when Ed Chambers, Alinsky's successor as the director of the IAF, hatched the idea to build upon the ties of community that did still exist among most Americans. Those were found mostly in the churches and other voluntary associations. It was in churches, especially, that grassroots leaders could be found, on parish councils and boards of elders and deacons, raising money, running meetings, and hammering out budgets—all the basic work of a democratic society.

So IAF set out to build church-based organizations across entire metropolitan areas. In these organizations, people became active through their congregation. Their black Baptist church remained black; their white Presbyterian church might remain white; their Catholic parish could remain Latino; but those three congregations and dozens of others like them, could join together in a triracial citywide network to act on the values and interests they held in common—values such as nurturing children, achieving social justice, or creating broad-based economic development.

In words that three decades later ring with prophecy, Chambers wrote in the late 1970s of the need for such organizations: "The economic and political middle of this country is being sucked dry by a vacuum—a vacuum of power and values. Into that vacuum have moved the huge corporations, mass media and 'benevolent' government. . . ." Chambers said this occurred because "the churches and unions were not prepared for the institutional arrangements and technologies that have overwhelmed us. . . . Without effective institutional power of their own, families and churches withdraw, backbite [and] blame each other."

Saul Alinsky's old rules for community organizing were based on the idea that people should be gathered on the basis of their shared material self-interest. The new generation of organizers recognized that the way people conceive their self-interest is itself shaped by their values. People value an adequate standard of living and education, which are plainly material interests, but they also value freedom, dignity, and responsibility. In the arena of family and local community, values and interests intersect. An adequate standard of living requires economic development that will benefit the entire community. Education for their own children is, for most people, inextricably tied to the success of the public school systems.

Ernesto Cortes, who built one of the first church-based IAF organizations in San Antonio, Texas, talks about the conjunction between "the world as it should be," ruled by love, and "the world as it is," ruled by power. Both love and power "come from God," Cortes said. "They are both part of creation." But love without power is mere sentiment. And power without love is oppressive and greedy. Church-based community organizations try to keep the two worlds in balance by using the power of numbers to work for policies based upon communally-held Judeo-Christian values.

Today there are literally hundreds of these organizations in every part of the country. IAF is still the biggest, but four other networks of church-based community organizations have arisen, using variations of the same model. These involve almost 2,000 congregations with more than 1.5 million members. And all of these organizations are interracial to the core.

PICO (Pacific Institute for Community Organizing), a network that began on the West Coast reported several years ago that its membership was 38 percent Hispanic, 33 percent white, 21 percent black, and 7 percent Asian. PICO also found that its member families were 37 percent working class, 29 percent middle class, and 12 percent low income. IAF says simply that the racial makeup of its organizations represents that of the areas in which they are located and that its center of gravity is in working class, working poor and lower-middle-class congregations, with the frequent involvement of middle and upper-middle-class supporters. In fact, IAF will only send an organizer into an area when an organizing committee of sponsoring congregations has been assembled that represents the religious and racial makeup of the community. The IAF Web site says it this way:

> We experience the joy of relating to people unlike ourselves, both within and outside of our organizations. We learn about the richness of other racial and ethnic and religious groups in an environment of mutual respect and regard. We watch new homeowners turn the key on the home of their dreams, children graduate with honors after four fulfilling years, grandmothers walk with confidence through lobbies once ruled by gangs, working people take home a wage that supports family life, whole communities rebuilt and renewed.

Each church-based community organization selects the issues for its city, based upon extensive canvassing of members. As the IAF Web site description suggests, these tend to focus on bread-and-butter concerns that sometimes bring the churches into alliance with the local establishment and sometimes lead to confrontation. In the mid-1990s, IAF-affiliated organizations in Baltimore and New York set out to attack declining wages with "living wage" campaigns. They pushed city councils to enact laws requiring any company doing business with the city government to pay a "living wage" in the neighborhood of $8-$10 per hour. Those campaigns succeeded, and now one hundred cities across the country have living wage laws. The Charlotte, North Carolina, church-based organization called Helping Empower Local People (HELP) contributed to the defeat of a referendum to spend $200 million in taxpayer money for a new professional sports stadium because the city council had failed to pass a "living wage" law that would ensure workers at the publicly-funded stadium earned at least $9 an hour.

Other church-based community organizations have focused with equal success on improving public schools, building affordable housing, and designing job training programs. The key is that issues are chosen that can be seen to benefit the entire community. Even when disproportionately poor blacks or Hispanics might benefit most, say from a job-training program, the issues are still defined nonracially through their broad benefit to the common good. The point is for people to build new relationships across racial lines by working together on what they have themselves identified as their common concerns. In fact, church-based community organizations generally avoid issues, such as local affirmative action programs, that resist nonracial definition. Member congregations are, of course, free to take stands on those issues through other channels, and they often do.

Relationships of Solidarity

Researcher Mark Warren has interviewed grassroots leaders from Allied Communities of Tarrant (ACT), the triracial IAF-affiliated organization in the Fort Worth, Texas, area about their experiences. He reports that "leaders from all three racial groups report that [their] involvement has led them to build new and deeper relationships" across racial lines.

Rosemary Galdiano is a Hispanic lay leader who, when interviewed, was chair of ACT's Health Care Action Team. She told Warren that she had become comfortable around whites when she attended the University of Texas–Austin. But before becoming involved with ACT she had been afraid of the black community. "Growing up in Fort Worth," she said, "my experience with the African-American community was negative. My father is very prejudiced. In high school racial tension was very high. There was a riot in school. I became afraid at school. I saw hate and it frightened me. We never mixed after that.... This organization changed my fear and misunderstanding with the black community by working together on a practical level. Working a phone bank, you begin to develop relationships, develop trust and begin to depend on each other."

Joyce Oliver, an African-American leader of ACT, told Warren that relationships built through the community organization are qualitatively different from those found on a job. "On the job," she said, "you just do a job. In ACT, you sit down and learn their values, how they feel. You begin to share, build a bond. Because it's church-based, if you say we're all children of God, it will prove that. It will change the way you look at other races, or else you'll leave. And some do."

Warren noted that ACT made a point of varying the location of meetings in different parts of the city, bringing leaders into the neighborhoods of other racial groups. Juanita Cisneros, a Hispanic leader, lives in a predominantly Anglo middle-class community. When she got involved with ACT, she signed on for the Job Training Action Team out of concern for her two sons' futures. "One of reasons I stayed with [the job training team] is that my husband and I grew up in poor families," Cisneros said. "We put ourselves through school and we have good jobs, feel secure. But I've been disappointed that even though we gave our kids all they wanted, my son didn't go to college. So at 24 he finds himself working at $6 or $6.50 per hour, and he has a baby to support. He still lives with us.... If you don't go to college, there is a lack of opportunity for good paying jobs."

"Job team meetings," Cisneros found, "were in the black part of town. I always went, but I felt uneasy, due to the high crime rate there. I would try to go with someone else. . . . Black people, the men especially, I've met in ACT are all gentlemen. I wouldn't hesitate to go anywhere with them."

Reverend Terry Boggs, a white ACT leader, told Warren that "everything changes because of relationships [built in ACT]. I can't write off a part of the city anymore because I know those people and have worked with them."

These church-based community organizations don't have visibility on the national scene. They don't have a flashy media strategy. You don't see them on CNN or even on CSPAN 2. But they are making a difference from New York to Los Angeles, with vital organizations in Atlanta, Chicago, New Orleans, San Antonio, Phoenix, and more than a hundred other cities scattered in between. While the eyes of mass media are on racial division, these organizations are quietly building permanent structures of interracial unity and solidarity.

Church-based community organizing is a practical expression of the ideals of solidarity and commitment to the common good that are contained in Catholic social teaching. It is a strategy that integrates a Judeo-Christian vision of justice and equality with the practical workings of democracy and community life. It does this by building on commonly shared interests and values across lines of race, ethnicity and income. It is promoting reconciled interracial relationships and working for social and economic policies that will increase interracial solidarity. Church-based community organizations are one of the main places where Americans—black, white and brown—are rising to common ground and building institutions that can move beyond racism, while continuing to value the gifts of ethnic and cultural identity.

Source Notes

Preface

"A Nation within a Nation. An Interview with Eugene Rivers." *Sojourners Magazine,* March-April 1998.

1. Does Race Still Matter?

Joint Center for Economic and Political Studies. *Income and Poverty among African Americans,* http://www.jointcenter.org/2004election/CBC-health-briefs/Economic+Brief.pdf

Congressional Black Caucus Foundation. *State of the Black Economy,* http://www.cbcfinc.org/CPAR/research.html

Frontline. http://www.pbs.org/wgbh/pages/frontline/shows/sats/etc/gap.html

Marjorie Suchocki. "Original Sin Revisited." *Process Studies* Vol. 20, Number 4, Winter, 1991. http://www.religion-online.org/showarticle.asp?title=2817

Bill Wylie-Kellermann. "Exorcising an American Demon." *Sojourners* March–April 1998.

2. What Is Racism?

Joel Kovel. *White Racism: A Psychohistory.* New York: Columbia University Press, 1984.

Aaron Kinney. "Why Did False Tales of Rape, Shootings and Murder Flood out of New Orleans in the Wake of Katrina?" http://dir.salon.com/story/news/feature/2005/10/24/katrina_horror/index.html

3. The Original Wedge Issue

Warren M. Billings, ed. *The Old Dominion in the Seventeenth Century: A Documentary History of Virginia, 1606-1689.* Chapel Hill: University of North Carolina Press, 1975.

Warren M. Billings. "The Cases of Fernando and Elizabeth Rey: A Note on the Status of Blacks in 17th Century Virginia." *William and Mary Quarterly* 1973.

Wesley Frank Craven. *The Southern Colonies in the Seventeenth Century: 1607–1689*. Baton Rouge: Louisiana State University Press, 1949.

William Waller Henning, ed. *The Laws of Virginia*. New York: R. & W. & G. Partow, 1823.

Edmund S. Morgan. *American Slavery, American Freedom: The Ordeal of Colonial Virginia*. New York: W.W. Norton, 1975.

Thomas Jefferson Wertenbaker. *Patrician and Plebian in Virginia*. New York: Russell & Russell, 1958.

Dave Marsh. *Glory Days: Bruce Springsteen in the 1980s*. New York: Pantheon, 1987.

Howard Zinn. *A People's History of the United States*. New York: Harpercollins: 1980.

Richard Boyer and Herbert Morais. *Labor's Untold Story*. New York: United Electrical, Radio and Machine Workers of America, 1955.

Barbara Fields. "Ideology and Race in American History," in J. Morgan Kousser, ed. *Region, Race and Reconstruction: Essays in Honor of C. Vann Woodward*. New York: Oxford University Press, 1982.

C. Vann Woodward. *Origins of the New South*. Baton Rouge: Louisiana State University Press, 1955.

———. *Tom Watson: Agrarian Rebel*. New York: Rinehart & Company, 1938.

Danny Duncan Collum. *Black and White Together*. Maryknoll, N.Y.: Orbis Books, 1996.

4. What Did White Christians Do?

Richard Reddie. "Atlantic Slave Trade and Abolition." BBC Religion & Ethics. http://www.bbc.co.uk/religion/religions/christianity/history/slavery_1.shtml

BBC. "Church Apologises for Slave Trade." http://news.bbc.co.uk/1/hi/uk/4694896.stm

Ian Frederick Finseth. "'Liquid Fire within Me': Language, Self and Society in Transcendentalism and Early Evangelicalism, 1820–1860." M.A. Thesis in English, University of Virginia, August 1995, http://xroads.virginia.edu/~MA95/finseth/thesis.html

Donald W. Dayton. Excerpt from *Discovering An Evangelical Heritage*. Hendrickson Publishers,1992, http://www.cscoweb.org/dayton.html

Editorial. "History of Slaveholding, Racism Calls for Amends." *National Catholic Reporter*, November 24, 2000.

5. The Third Great Awakening

Henry Hampton, Producer. *Eyes on the Prize*. Boston: Blackside Productions, television series, 1986.

William McGuire King. "Shadows of the Social Gospel: White Mainliners in the Civil Rights Struggle." *Christian Century* April 6, 1994.

Milton Viorst. *Fire in the Streets: America in the 1960s.* New York: Simon & Schuster, 1979.

6. The Racial Landscape of the Twenty-first Century

Wayne Washington. *Minneapolis–St. Paul Star Tribune,* September 26, 1996, http://www.americancivilrightsreview.com/civilrightspositivenews1.html

Henry Louis Gates. *Frontline* interview, http://www.pbs.org/wgbh/pages/frontline/shows/race/interviews/gates.html

Jonathan Kozol. *Savage Inequalities.* New York: Harper Perennial, 1992.

The Futures Project. "The Growing Divide: Making the Case for All to Succeed," http://www.futuresproject.org/publications/FactSheet1.pdf

Center for Responsible Lending (CRL). "Payday Lenders Prey on African-American Neighborhoods," http://www.consumeraffairs.com/news04/2005/payday_lenders.html

"Minority Car Buyers Sue Major Auto Loan Companies," http://www.gdblegal.com/press.php?menuItem=5&article=23

The Pew Center for People and the Press. "The Black and White of Public Opinion: Did the Racial Divide in Attitudes about Katrina Mislead Us?" http://people-press.org/commentary/display.php3?AnalysisID=121

"Racial Profiling: Old and New." http://www.aclu.org/racialjustice/racialprofiling/index.html

The Urban League. "The State of Black America," http://nul.org/thestateof blackamerica.html

7. Where to Start? Sources for a Faithful Response to Racism

G. McLeod Bryan. "Theology in Overalls: The Imprint of Clarence Jordan." *Sojourners* December 1979.

Joyce Hollyday. "The Dream That Has Endured: Clarence Jordan and Koinonia." *Sojourners* December 1979.

Clarence Jordan. *The Cotton Patch Version of Matthew and John.* New York: Association Press, 1970.

Clarence Jordan. *The Cotton Patch Version of Luke and Acts.* New York: Association Press, 1969.

Rene Girard. *The Scapegoat.* Baltimore: Johns Hopkins University Press, 1986.

James Cone. "Black Liberation Theology and Black Catholics: A Critical Conversation." *Theological Studies* December 20.

Cyprian Davis. "Black Catholic Theology: A Historical Perspective." *Theological Studies* December 2000.

U.S. Catholic Bishops. *Brothers and Sisters to Us* http://www.osjspm.org/ majordoc_us_bishops_statements_brothers_and_sisters.aspx

General Assembly of the Presbyterian Church (U.S.A.). *Facing Racism: A Vision of the Beloved Community* 1999. http://www.pcusa.org/oga/publications/ facing-racism.pdf

World Council of Churches Central Committee. *Being Church and Overcoming Racism: It's Time for Transformative Justice* September 2002. http://www2.wcccoe.org/ccdocuments.nsf/index/plen-4-en.html

The House of Bishops of the Episcopal Church. *The Sin of Racism: A Call to Covenant* March 2006. http://www.episcopalchurch.org/3654_73047_ ENG_HTM.htm

Evangelical Lutheran Church in America Churchwide Assembly. *Freed in Christ* 1993. http://www.elca.org/socialstatements/freedinchrist/

Pontifical Commission Justice and Peace. *The Church and Racism: Toward a More Fraternal Society*, http://www3.villanova.edu/mission/journal/ racism/pcjpraci.htm

8. The First Step: Confession

John Conyers, Jr. "Briefing on the Impact of Slavery on Today's African Americans," http://www.house.gov/conyers/news_reparations.htm

Dylan T. Lovan. "The Invisible Press." *The Jackson Sun*. 2000, http://orig. jacksonsun.com/civilrights/sec6_ourstory.shtml

Crystal Keel. "Still No Forty Acres, Still No Mule: Acknowledgment of Past Wrongs May Help Put African American Reparations in the Spotlight." *Black Issues in Higher Education* August 11, 2005.

Peter Smith. "Returning These People to Our History: Sisters of Loretto Honor Slaves." *Louisville Courier-Journal* August 1, 2000.

Peter Smith. "Nuns apologize for slave legacy." *Louisville Courier-Journal* December 4, 2000.

9. Pushing the Buttons

Ellis Cose. "Long after the Alarm Went Off." *Newsweek* March 14, 2005.

William Julius Wilson Interview, http://www.pbs.org/fmc/interviews/ wilson.htm

William Julius Wilson. *When Work Disappears*. New York: Vintage, 1997.

Roland Warren. "Marriage is Great Equalizer for Blacks."

USA Today January 5, 2006, http://www.usatoday.com/news/opinion/editorials/ 2006-01-05-warren-edit_x.htm

Review of *Climbing Jacob's Ladder: The Enduring Legacy of African-American Families* by Andrew Billingsley. Reviewed by Arlie Hochschild,

http://query.nytimes.com/gst/fullpage.html?res=9F0CE4DC1030F933A
15755C0A965958260

Christopher Jencks. "Is the American Underclass Growing." In Jencks and
Peterson, eds., *Urban Underclass*. Washington, DC: Brookings Institution, 1991.

Gary S. Tschoepe. "Rational Choice and Out-of-Wedlock Births among
African American Females: The Influence of AFDC and Unemployment." *Social Science Journal* 1999.

Sourcebook of Criminal Justice Statistics Online, www.albany.edu/sourcebook

The Council of Economic Advisors. *Changing America: Indicators of Social and
Economic Well-being by Race and Hispanic Origin*, http://www.access.
gpo.gov/eop/ca/pdfs/toc.pdf

"Off Balance: Youth, Race & Crime in the News." Prepared by Lori Dorfman,
Berkeley Media Studies Group, Public Health Institute, Vincent
Schiraldi and Justice Policy Institute, http://www.buildingblocksfor
youth.org/media/media.html

Leadership Conference on Civil Rights. "Civil Rights 101: Criminal Justice,"
http://www.civilrights.org/research_center/civilrights101/crimjustice.html

Human Rights Watch. "Incarceration and Race," http://www.hrw.org/reports/
2000/usa/Rcedrg00-01.htm

10. Racial Remedies? Affirmative Action and Reparations

Ronald Roach. "Class-Based Affirmative Action." *Black Issues in Higher Education* June 19, 2003.

Cornel West. *Race Matters*. New York: Vintage, 1994.

"What's At Stake? Why Are Reparations Controversial?" http://academic.
udayton.edu/race/02rights/repara29b.htm

Glenn C. Loury. "Black and White: Why Reparations for African-Americans
Are Intellectually Indefensible." *Forbes* February 4, 2002.

"Slave Reparations." *Religion and Ethics Newsweekly*. Features interviews with
Wendy Kaminer, Charles Ogletree, Randall Robinson, Glenn C. Loury and
others, http://www.pbs.org/wnet/religionandethics/week419/feature.html

Adolf Reed. "The Case against Reparations." *The Progressive* December 2000.

11. What Next? Building Solidarity

Office of Racial Justice. Archdiocese of Chicago. http://www.archchicago.org/
departments/racial_justice/racial_justice.shtm

Christopher John Farley. "The Gospel of Diversity." *Time* April 24, 1995.
http://www.time.com/time/magazine/article/0,9171,982839,00.html

Nibs Stroupe and Inez Fleming. *While We Run This Race*. Orbis Books, 1995.

John D. Filiatreau. "Who Me? Prejudiced?" *Presbyterians Today* September
       2000. www.pcusa.org/today/archive/features/feat0009.htm
Don Beisswenger. "O Lord Hold Our Hands." *Hospitality* May 2003.
       http://opendoorcommunity.org/HospMay03.pdf
www.oakhurstpresbyterian.org

12. Rising to Common Ground

The Industrial Areas Foundation, http://www.industrialareasfoundation.org/
PICO National Network, http://www.piconetwork.org/
Mark R. Warren. "Creating a Multi-racial Democratic Community: Case
       Study of the Texas Industrial Areas Foundation" The Civic Practices
       Network, http://www.tresser.com/iafin.htm